The Business of Child Care

Management and Financial Strategies

Gail Jack

DELMAR
CENGAGE Learning

Australia • Brazil • Japan • Korea • Mexico • Singapore • Spain • United Kingdom • United States

DELMAR
CENGAGE Learning™

The Business of Child Care:
Management and Financial Strategies
Gail Jack

Vice President, Career Education SBU:
  Dawn Gerrain

Director of Editorial: Sherry Gomoll

Acquisitions Editor: Erin O'Connor

Editorial Assistant: Ivy Ip

Director of Production: Wendy
  A. Troeger

Production Editor: J. P. Henkel

Technology Project Manager:
  Joseph Saba

Director of Marketing: Wendy
  E. Mapstone

Channel Manager: Donna J. Lewis

Cover Design: Joe Villanova

For product information and technology assistance, contact us at
Cengage Learning Customer & Sales Support, 1-800-354-9706

For permission to use material from this text or product,
submit all requests online at **www.cengage.com/permissions**
Further permissions questions can be emailed to
permissionrequest@cengage.com

Library of Congress Cataloging-in-Publication Data

Jack, Gail.
   The business of child care : management and financial strategies / by Gail Jack.
      p. cm.
   Includes bibliographical references and index.
   ISBN-13: 978-1-4018-5180-4
   ISBN-10: 1-4018-5180-0
   1. Day care centers—Administration. I. Title.
HQ778.5.J33 2005
362.71'2'068—dc22   2004051721

Delmar
10 Davis Drive
Belmont, CA 94002-3098
USA

Cengage Learning is a leading provider of customized learning solutions with office locations around the globe, including Singapore, the United Kingdom, Australia, Mexico, Brazil, and Japan. Locate your local office at: **international.cengage.com/region**

Cengage Learning products are represented in Canada by Nelson Education, Ltd.

For your lifelong learning solutions, visit **delmar.cengage.com**
Visit our corporate website at **cengage.com**

Join us on the Web at **EarlyChildEd.delmar.cengage.com**

Printed in the United States of America
11 16 15

Contents

Dedication   iv
Preface   v
Acknowledgments   vi

CHAPTER 1
**The Child Care Administrator:
Who You Are, How You Manage** 1
Management Styles 1
Working with Staff and Why We Should Care
about Our Staff 5
Working with Parents and Why We Should
Care about Our Parents 8
Working with Management and Why We
Should Care about Our Managers 10
References 12

CHAPTER 2
Enrollment, Staffing, and Tuition Fees . . . 13
The Importance of Enrollment 13
Determining Your Capacity 14
Maintaining High Enrollment 16
Determining Your Fee Structure 18
Putting It All Together and Keeping It There 30
References 30
Helpfull Web Sites 31

CHAPTER 3
**Staffing: A Guide to Recruitment
and Retention** 32
Making Your Program a Good Place to Work 32
Determining What You Need, What You Want,
and What You Can Afford 32
Finding Qualified Staff 37
Hiring 39
Personnel Policies and Procedures 42
Other Good Things for Staff 47

References 49
Helpful Web Sites 49

CHAPTER 4
The Budget 50
The Basic Budget 50
Expense Components 52
Revenue Components 62
What Next? 71

CHAPTER 5
The Budget as a Planning Tool 72
Using Your Budget 72
Estimating Monthly Budget Amounts 72
Tracking Revenue and Expenses Month to Month 79
Understanding Variances and Problem Solving 83
Thoughts on Cost Savings 100

CHAPTER 6
Financial Record Keeping 101
The Reasons Why We Want to Keep Good
Financial Records 101
Accrual versus Cash Basis of Accounting 102
What Documents to Keep 103
How to Keep Your Financial Records 111
Fiscal Year-End 118
Financial Record Keeping 101 118
Reference 119

CHAPTER 7
The Decision-Making Process 120
Who Is Making the Decisions? 120
What Is Inclusive Decision Making? 122
What Inclusive Decision Making Looks Like:
Four Examples 123

Teaching Yourself to Let Go. 127

Reference. 127

APPENDIX A
**Employee Performance
Review Forms** 128

Staff Pre-Conference Questionnaire. 128

Goals Planning. 129

Staff Action Plan. 130

APPENDIX B
Spreadsheet Terminology 131

APPENDIX C
Useful Web Sites 134

Glossary 135

Index 136

*This book is dedicated to Ann Zondor Hentschel. Without her support,
encouragement, and good humor I would never have
started a career in early childhood education.*

Preface

This book grew out of a love for the job of executive director of a large nonprofit child care center on a university campus and the inspiration of a gifted early childhood visionary who was my first supervisor in a child care center. Its focus is on helping those early childhood professionals who will be administering a child care program in their career or who now find themselves managing one. This book will help you understand the issues of running a business and managing people and budgets. It will help you get out of your office and back into your classrooms with your staff and families.

With a business background and a master's degree in business administration from Stanford University, my working experience is rooted in the corporate world. I was a financial manager before starting my career in early childhood. I worked as an administrator in child care for the past 12 years and in addition was the owner of a consulting company for small businesses. This background gives me a unique perspective on what it takes to manage a child care business.

None of the material in this book deals with curriculum for young children or with young children at all. It is a book about running a business that happens to be child care. You already know how to best serve young children and their families, but you may not know what is meant by the accrual basis of accounting. *The Business of Child Care* is written for early childhood professionals both in the classroom and on the job. It can help the student taking administrative classes in college. It can help the director of a program that has a business manager: that director is still responsible for the overall fiscal integrity of the program and must understand and guide the financial management of the program. It can help a director working for a child care corporation who must understand how a budget functions and how to retain qualified teachers. It can help a family child care provider: her work is a business and she should know how to keep track of revenue and expenses and plan for the future as well as how to recruit and retain employees. The goal of this book is to teach you the skills you need to manage human and financial resources, how to

plan for a financially stable enterprise, and how to complete your business tasks more quickly and accurately, with greater understanding and more enjoyment by focusing on the most essential tasks of a child care administrator. A brief description of chapter topics is included below.

The material is presented in a straightforward, concise manner with charts in every chapter. You will find TIPS where I share insights on important issues and HINTS that guide you toward a greater understanding of the concepts presented. Numerous examples taken from my experiences as a center director are included in the story boxes; these examples illustrate how the principles work in real-life situations. Information boxes give greater detail about selected topics.

The CD included at the back contains most of the charts and spreadsheets in the book and blank templates from which you can design forms to fit your particular child care program. By copying a spreadsheet into your own software and then modifying headings, rows, and columns, adding formulas and dollar amounts, you will create your organization's unique format to save as a file on your computer. The original spreadsheet template on the CD will not change.

Chapter 1: The Child Care Administrator: Who You Are, How You Manage. There are many different management styles and books on "how to" manage. This chapter discusses typical management styles, but stresses the importance of knowing who you are and managing authentically. The chapter includes tips on communicating with staff, parents, upper management, and boards of directors.

Chapter 2: Enrollment, Staffing, and Tuition Fees. The key to a successful child care program is maintaining full enrollment. Chapter 2 discusses why enrollment is the vital factor for a financially stable program, the relationship between enrollment and staffing levels, and how to facilitate high enrollment even in difficult economic times. The development of a fee structure is explored in detail.

Chapter 3: Staffing: A Guide to Recruitment and Retention. Staffing can make or break a quality child care program. Monitoring the costs of staff compensation is the most important factor in controlling a center's expenses. This chapter discusses ways to attract quality staff to a program, design clear and usable compensation systems, and design programs to retain staff.

Chapter 4: The Budget.   Chapter 4 contains an easy-to-follow, step-by-step discussion of how to create a usable budget. The chapter contains many examples and spreadsheets for the reader. It also highlights the importance of tuition revenue and staff salaries and benefits as the two most important components of the budget.

Chapter 5: The Budget as a Planning Tool.   As important as designing a budget for a child care program is using that budget as a management tool. Chapter 5 focuses on how a budget is used to track actual income and expenses through the budget year, and how decisions are made based on a center's performance against its budget.

Chapter 6: Financial Record Keeping.   This chapter delineates the nuts and bolts of keeping financial records.

Chapter 7: The Decision-Making Process.   In this chapter we take a look at how inclusive decision making works and why it is a good model for child care administrators.

Appendix A provides employee performance review forms, Appendix B lists spreadsheet terminology, and Appendix C gives useful Web sites. A glossary of key terms (which are highlighted in boldface type throughout the book) is found at the end of this volume.

This is a relatively short book. You don't have time to read through page after page before getting to the point of your question. You need a book to which you can turn as a reference when you are developing your budget, or balancing your books, or hiring a new teacher.

The Business of Child Care is intended to be your business reference: write in it, dog-ear the pages you want to get to quickly, attach stickies that label the pages you may refer to frequently. And, always remember, your true focus is providing high quality care to children and families and to continue to enjoy and thrive in the work you do.

ACKNOWLEDGMENTS

The author would like to thank the following reviewers, enlisted by Delmar, for their helpful suggestions and constructive criticism.

Jeanne Barker
Tallahassee Community College
Tallahassee, Florida

Toni Cacace-Beshears
Tidewater Community College
Chesapeake, Virginia

Elaine Camerin, Ed.D.
Daytona Beach Community College
Daytona Beach, Florida

Kay Crowder
Ivy Tech State College
Ft. Wayne, Indiana

Vicki Folds, Ed.D.
Vice President of Education
Tutor Time Learning Systems
Boca Raton, Florida

Jody Martin
Educational Consultant
Golden, Colorado

CHAPTER 1

The Child Care Administrator: Who You Are, How You Manage

MANAGEMENT STYLES

In a book about the business of administering a child care facility you may expect to find a discussion or explanation of how you should behave as a manager of your program. You might anticipate reading the dos and don'ts of managing, or lists of management secrets. You can find such lists in almost any business management book on the shelves of your bookstore or library. There are endless numbers of such books, and an endless array of recommended management strategies, some coming in and out of fashion through the decades.

What Others Tell Us

Stephen Covey's book *The Seven Habits of Highly Effective People* (1989) is a good example of this kind of book. In it, Mr. Covey describes seven rules to live by in order to be successful in your life and work. Before Mr. Covey, in the 1980s, Tom Peters was the guru of management advice for a while; in *In Search of Excellence* (1982) Mr. Peters delineates eight basics of management excellence. Although these books are located in the business section of your library or bookstore, they can be adapted to the work we do in child care because we manage human and financial resources like every other business. You may find some very useful insights in these books written by individuals who have run corporations or have been consultants to the heads of corporations.

For me, however, the points of view in these books never really resonated with how I felt I was performing as a manager. It never felt right to adopt someone else's way of managing. It never felt *authentic* and I was never comfortable with trying to behave like someone else in order to do my job well.

Rather than read management books and then adopt someone else's management style, I believe it is more instructive to learn about all of the different styles of managing observed in the workplace. Then we need to understand where our own natural style fits into the range of styles. In an article published in the *Harvard Business Review* in March–April 2000, Daniel Goleman (the author of *Emotional Intelligence* [1995]) discusses research conducted by the consulting firm of Hay/McBer, with which he is associated. The researchers observed a random sample of nearly 4,000 business executives out of a database of 20,000 executives. "The research found six distinct leadership styles, each springing from different components of emotional intelligence" (p. 78). The six leadership styles that they observed and their characteristics in brief are

- coercive: demanding immediate compliance
- authoritative: mobilizing people toward a vision
- affiliative: creating harmony and building emotional bonds
- democratic: consensus building
- pacesetting: do as I do: modeling high standards
- coaching: developing people for the future

The research team went on to measure how each of these styles affects the **organizational climate,** i.e., the organization's working environment. Two of the leadership styles the team had named, coercive and pacesetting, had only negative effects on all the components of climate, while the other four styles—authoritative, affiliative, democratic, and coaching—were mostly positive in their effects. The research further concluded that "the leaders with the best results do not rely on only one leadership style; *they use most of them in a given week*—seamlessly and in different measure—depending on the business situation" (pp. 78–79). Interestingly, the positive effects that some of the styles, or combination of styles, had on the organizational climate were also positively tied to the financial results of these organizations.

✓Hint

Flexibility and fluidity in working with your employees is good for your organization.

Using this approach to understanding people who work in management positions seems to be more effective and gives us a truer picture of ourselves than trying to fit everyone into one "best" style of managing. Your style may look like one or more of the styles named above. It is a style that is already yours, and unless your style leans too much toward being coercive or pacesetting, it probably works pretty well.

I like to think about styles of managing as ranging along a spectrum from "directive" to "nondirective" (terms used by Carl Glickman in his 1981 monograph, "Developmental Supervision: Alternative Practices for Helping Teachers") or from "controlling" to "permissive." In terms of the leadership styles named by Goleman, a permissive manager uses democratic or coaching techniques to supervise his staff, while a controlling manager is coercive or pacesetting in her approach to staff supervision.

Figure 1–1 is a representation of this spectrum of management styles. Our controlling manager is one who makes all the decisions; he tells everyone else exactly how to do their job. He also always knows exactly what everyone is doing at all times. Teachers are instructed how, what, and when to teach in their classrooms and they must clear all decisions through their supervisor. From the dictionary, we learn that control means "to exercise restraining or directing influence over . . . to have power over . . . to rule." (Webster, p. 245)

At the other end of the managing spectrum is the permissive manager who allows everyone to make their own decisions and set their own goals. She is probably more concerned about her employees' feelings than about what is getting accomplished. She does not know what her employees are doing at any particular time and does not give any specific directions to her staff. In a child care program, this is an administrator who allows

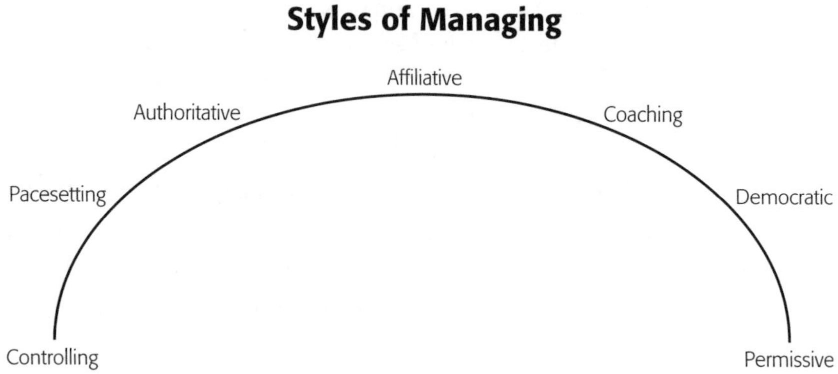

Styles of Managing

FIGURE 1–1 Styles of Managing

each classroom to develop its own curriculum and its own daily schedule and shifts for each team member.

Your fundamental style is somewhere along this continuum. The name you give it is the one that you use as your answer to the interview question, "What is your management style?" I am not suggesting that you behave the same every day, in every situation, with every employee. Remember, it is most effective to move flexibly from one mode to another as the situation requires. As you interact with others throughout your day, you are continually moving back and forth along the managing spectrum. You probably already do this even without thinking about it. *In general*, people tend to be either more or less controlling, or more or less permissive, or somewhere in between, just as their personality tends to be pretty consistent. Rather than having different *styles* with different employees, I believe each person has one fundamental style, but can use different *tools* or *techniques,* such as coaching or consensus building, depending on the situation and the individual.

How We Develop Our Style and What It's Called

I've always considered books that give you advice on how to manage people to be much like cookbooks. You would never use only one cookbook, making all the recipes in it and *only* those recipes. You have several cookbooks, and you also find recipes in newspapers and magazines and trade recipes with friends. Your recipes are collected from many sources. They have been tried and tested in your home and you have determined which recipes you like and which ones you don't like. Some recipes work for certain special occasions, and other recipes work well for serving particular people.

It's the same with management advice: No one book really tells you everything you need to know about being an administrator. Some advice from one book may work well in a particular situation with a particular employee, while you may have to use another "recipe" when working with a different employee. Another management technique may be one learned from a respected colleague or from a workshop attended.

Over a period of time, as we collect management tools that work for us, like the recipes we enjoy, we add to our collection. We keep adding techniques we pick up along the way, and maybe we eliminate some techniques from our repertoire because they no longer work well or because we have new tools that work better. Then one day, even without realizing it, we have amassed a collection of tools we use for managing the people who work for us. "Our style" may not be the same every day, or may not be the same with every employee, but there usually is some consistency in how we relate to the people we supervise and how we use these tools. It comes from the core of who we are. In his article, "Using the Right Personality Style" (1992), Daniel Tomal refers to the work of Carl Jung, a Swiss psychoanalyst who lived in the late nineteenth and early twentieth centuries. Jung believed that everyone is one of four genetically determined personality styles that Mr. Tomal labels "intuitor," "feeler," "thinker," and "doer." The characteristics of these styles are the following:

intuitor: idealistic, idea oriented, unrealistic, dogmatic, creative, imaginative, original, conceptualizer

feeler: warm, sensitive, loyal, empathetic, introspective, sentimental, impulsive

thinker: organized, structured, prudent, conservative, objective, analytical, rational, overly cautious, nondynamic, controlled, rigid

doer: results oriented, assertive, pragmatic, quick thinker, action oriented, directive, self-involved (Tomal, p. 13).

As we go about our work and interact with the people on our staff or the parents in our community, Tomal believes that we can use this information about our own and our coworkers' styles to become more effective managers. "A good supervisor needs to understand and appreciate contrasting styles" (p. 13). If I know that I tend to have a "doer" personality, I can learn that not everyone I work with will be as results oriented as I am. If a head teacher is more concerned about the feelings of his teammates, he may be reluctant to face a team member who consistently comes in late. But by understanding how his personality type or style affects his work with others, we can find a better way to coach him in dealing with a problem team member. We need to be flexible in communicating with others by using all the styles described above in response to the predominate styles of our staff members.

Hint

By learning about each employee's personality style, you can discover more effective ways to coach them and develop their skills.

What Makes Your Style Unique

Your way of managing people is unique; it reflects who you are. Although you can learn new techniques to help you do your job better and better understand your own performance, your management style develops from your personality and evolves naturally over time.

Who You Are.   In all your interpersonal interactions, and especially in the field of early childhood where you work so closely with children, parents, and coworkers, it is vital to understand your own background and how it is reflected in your work. Your childhood experiences affect how you think about caring for and teaching children; your relations with your parents affect how you interact with the families in your program. The experiences you've had, or your lack of experience, with individuals of different ethnicities and cultures affects how you perceive people who are different from you. Your own culture influences what you believe to be the best for children and families. What kind of school environment you experienced as a child, or the experience your own children have had or are having, can affect your approach to teaching. You have to know yourself and appreciate who you are and all you have learned through the years and acknowledge the influence your past has on how you perform today.

How You Manage.   Thus your own personality and your particular background, combined with the management tools you've picked up along the way, blend together to form your unique management style. Because no two people have the same background, no two will have the same management style. You can learn to be a better, more effective manager. Knowing yourself is the first step. Learning new techniques is the second step and this learning continues throughout your life. You also continue to learn by **reflecting** on your experiences as an administrator.

Reflection is the process of psychologically stepping back from your work to examine how you feel about what you did and how others feel about what you did, and to look at the results of your actions. It is a quiet moment or two that you take to try to understand your actions and motivations in managing a situation the way you did. It is how you learn to do things better or differently the next time, or, perhaps, how you can understand your own biases that you may be reluctant to acknowledge. You can write notes to yourself that describe why, what, and how you made a decision, and what your feelings were through the process. Maybe you are already able to make notes about what went wrong or how you would handle the situation differently in the future. Perhaps you realize that you have left some things unsaid or unheard, and are then able to rectify the omission. It is a process that accepts the mistakes you may make and helps you learn from them.

WORKING WITH STAFF AND WHY WE SHOULD CARE ABOUT OUR STAFF

I suppose there is an obvious response to this issue, and I suppose some of us think there is no need even to raise this matter. After all, none of us would admit that we *don't* care about our staff. But, as obvious as it is that we all usually want to treat our staff well, child care administrators need to understand how important the well-being of their staff is to the well-being of their program. As pointed out by the Center for the Child Care Workforce in its (1998) booklet *Creating Better Child Care Jobs*, "Good Child Care Jobs = Good Care for Children." Based on research done over many years, we know that compensation and working conditions for staff are *the* most important factors in providing quality care for children. The center's longitudinal study (from 1994 to 2000 in three California communities), which was published in 2001 as *Then & Now* (Whitebook, Sakai, Gerber, & Howes), describes the effects of high staff turnover on the quality of care centers provide. Some of their important conclusions are stated below:

- "Centers paying higher wages are better able to retain qualified teachers." (vii)
- "Highly skilled and educated teaching staff are more likely to remain at their jobs if they earn higher than average wages, and work with a higher percentage of well-trained teaching staff who also remain on the job." (vii–viii)
- "The presence of a greater proportion of highly trained teaching staff in 2000 is the strongest predictor of whether a center can sustain quality improvements over time. Wages is [*sic*] also a significant predictor." (viii)

We know that being good to our staff not only makes us feel good and is the right thing to do, but it is the best thing we can do to achieve our ultimate goal of running a program that provides high quality care for children.

Know Your Staff

For the same reasons that it is important to know yourself and the influence your background has on your performance as an administrator, it is also important to get to know and understand the people working in your program. Each person brings a variety of different characteristics and personalities to their work that influences how they perform. If you are to use the management tools in your collection most effectively, you need to know which tools will work in which situations for which staff members. If you hope to "connect" with your staff, you'll want to understand their backgrounds, their families, and their philosophies about working with children. I recommend that administrators read through all the personnel files of their staff, even if you think you know someone well, and then meet individually with each employee to get to know them better. These meetings should be very informal, intended as "check-in meetings" so that you can learn how things are going for each staff member. Your goal is to develop a level of trust with your employees that allows them to feel comfortable talking to you about many issues. In turn, you want to be able to give them direct, sincere feedback in such a way that they can *hear* and *understand* you. And if they don't understand what you are saying, or don't agree with what you are saying, staff should feel comfortable in telling you that, too.

Ways to Improve Staff Performance

An administrator can progress a long way toward improving the performance of all of her staff just by getting to know them better. As they get to know you better and learn to trust that you really care about them as individuals, staff members will feel connected to the community you are trying to create in your program. This is called **buy-in,** where individuals buy into the job they are performing because they feel they are listened to and respected and have a part in determining the kind of environment in which they work. They feel they are an integral part of the community.

In a following chapter, we'll talk more about staff performance, performance evaluations, and dealing with poorly performing individuals. In general, administrators don't like to deal with these issues and tend to avoid individuals who may be causing problems in their programs. I know because I have done this myself. But we will all have occasion as administrators to need to know how to work with difficult or underperforming employees, and it can be done in a constructive way. These difficult issues do not go away by themselves. By failing to face them when they first come to your attention, you are only permitting them to become larger problems. Often the hardest issue, the most difficult challenge we face as managers, is disciplining members of our staff. Yet working through these issues can also ultimately be the most satisfying to us as we help an individual overcome her difficulties, or help an individual learn that child care many not be the right profession for her.

Organizational Climate: Making Your Program a Good Place to Work

The way we manage has a direct effect on the climate of our organization and that climate in turn influences how people feel about working for us. All the things we have talked about in relation to working with your staff can positively influence the climate of your workplace. We are talking about creating an atmosphere of trust in our program, one in which all individuals are valued and respected for what they bring into the community. We foster this atmosphere of trust by getting to know our staff as individuals and giving them easy access to us. We allow and encourage differences of opinion.

Another important aspect of creating an environment in which people enjoy working is the dissemination of information. I have always been an advocate of sharing with staff as much information as is possible and prudent. If, as an administrator, you trust the members of your staff as you want them to trust you, you should be comfortable in sharing information. If you are in a corporate program or in a Head Start program, your guidelines for the dissemination of information come from the management for which you work and you may have less control over what information you share. In other kinds of programs there is a lot of administrative information you can share openly, aside from some obvious exceptions. For example, I never publicize what particular teachers are earning, although I do make public the wage matrix from which everyone's salary is determined.

When information is freely shared with employees and parents in your community, they will be better prepared to participate when you need someone in the organization's community to help you make a decision. Staff and parents will know the facts and be less confused by rumors they have heard. They will not be surprised when you ask for their participation and already will be at least partially informed about the issues. In Chapter 7, I discuss the process of making decisions where we include staff and parents.

! TIP

Never underestimate the value of buy-in by your staff. It is a crucial component of developing a true community within your organization.

Rosa's Story

"Rosa" had been an employee of our center since the first day it opened. She was the head teacher in a preschool classroom. Rosa had witnessed the coming and going of eight directors in the center's ten-year history when I became the executive director. Even though I had been the center's business manager for the past three years and was a known entity to the staff, my role as director was new. As a long-term employee and well-respected teacher in the center, Rosa held a lot of informal power.

My relationship with Rosa was formal and polite. She did not share her feelings with me or bring issues to me to discuss, but instead maintained a close-knit teaching team that rarely participated in centerwide events. She was a dependable employee who provided her children with a rich and nurturing environment.

Over the three and a half years of my tenure as executive director, I was involved in several issues with Rosa concerning her teachers or families in her classroom. I worked with her in dealing with some very difficult and challenging children and meeting with their parents. I learned more about Rosa, about how she came into the early childhood profession, about her family, about where she was going on vacation.

I witnessed the gradual building of a trusting relationship with Rosa as she, little by little, opened up to me and began to voice her (sometimes dissenting) opinions more often in our monthly staff meetings. I saw her laugh more and open up to the other staff members in the center. I could sense that she was enjoying her job more and that we no longer needed to put on a polite façade when we met.

The development of our relationship made it possible for us to work through a very difficult situation together and move beyond it with our relationship still intact. We were interviewing applicants for a teaching position for her team. The preschool program coordinator and I conducted the initial screening interviews. Each final candidate for the position then came in to observe in the classroom for an hour and have a follow-up meeting with Rosa.

Rosa was very hard to please. In fact, she did not want any of the candidates we had selected as finalists for her team. The program coordinator and I met with Rosa and her team to discuss the candidates and review the pros and cons of each one. Rosa was clear that none of them was acceptable to her. I responded in the meeting that I disagreed with her and in spite of her opposition we might be hiring one of the candidates for her team. I explained my position at some length: needing to find someone for her classroom after many months of having an open position, the feelings of parents in the room who were tired of the many substitutes floating through, and my feeling we had found some very well qualified individuals from which to choose. We closed the meeting without making a decision.

Over the next few days I reviewed all of the information concerning the candidates, our budget, and the situation existing in a classroom with only two-thirds of a full, regular teaching team. I discussed all aspects with the program coordinator. In the end, I chose a candidate to hire for the position and informed Rosa of my decision. She was not happy to have a teacher hired for her team that she did not want. But, because of the solid relationship we had built between us, and the open discussion and deliberation about the candidates and hiring for the team, Rosa accepted my decision and my authority to make that decision. She was able to express her disagreement and at the same time she let me know she would try to make it work. She was able to trust that from my point of view it was the right decision to make.

In particular, I believe in talking openly about finances and the budget with all staff members. At my former program, I prepared a budget presentation at the first all-staff meeting of every academic year. The budget presentation was repeated annually. At monthly meetings I presented a brief update on the center's finances. This was the same information that went to our board of directors. When we were losing money, the staff knew it, and they knew why. When we had a surplus, the staff was also informed.

There are many advantages to the dissemination of this kind of information. Some of these advantages are

- ■ Full disclosure on financial issues puts a lid on rumors.
- ■ Staff who understand when and why a center has a deficit are more willing to help control spending.
- ■ Staff and parents who understand when and why a center has a deficit contribute ideas to help reduce the deficit.
- ■ Full disclosure helps build a sense of community in good times and in bad: "We're all in this together."

It is wonderful and amazing to see a community work together during a financial crisis. I believe if you have this kind of community, your program will be able to survive most disasters.

WORKING WITH PARENTS AND WHY WE SHOULD CARE ABOUT OUR PARENTS

Our families are the reason we exist as a business. Their concerns are our concerns. We adjust tuition fees and children's schedules to fit their needs in order to stay in business. The parents in our program are the most important adults in our children's lives. They play the primary role in their child's development. We must operate as a team with parents in order to provide each child with the support, consistency, and nurturing they all need for optimal development.

On a more selfish note, we should care about our parents because then they will care about us. Parents who are happy with the care they receive for their children are willing to give a little extra in time and money in order to ensure that kind of care will continue. They will talk about our program with their friends, family, and colleagues. They will respond positively when we ask for extra help on a workday, or for purchases on our wish list.

What Parents Need

As a parent and as a former director of a child care center, I believe all parents who put their children in the care of someone outside their family need to know their child is safe and well cared for while away from home. There are a lot of other things parents want for their children of course, and these things may differ from family to family. But the bottom line for all families is the safety of their child and the meeting of their child's basic needs, such as providing food, a place to sleep or rest, and toileting or diapering assistance.

Every program must meet the basic needs of care and provide a healthy and safe environment. Beyond this, you will add other things your program wants to provide. For example, home visits may be a key component of your program, or primary care groups. Providing enrichment to preschoolers in the form of gymnastics and music may be your center's specialty. In response to requests from parents, you may provide parent education seminars on such topics as "Limit Setting for Two-Year-Olds" and "Kindergarten Information." Our center incorporated a philosophy of "emergent curriculum" to foster the particular interests of each child.

Making Your Program a Good Place for Families

Now that you are providing a safe and healthy environment for children, meeting their basic needs, and you have added your program's special characteristics, you need to let your parents know what you do, how you do it, and why you do it. Communication with parents is essential. You will never have control over what is read, but you can control what is written and disseminated to parents. Communication should occur frequently and regularly and the most important information for parents should be repeated and sent out to them in various formats: newsletters, e-mails, flyers in children's cubbies, notices on doors to their classrooms.

All of this takes time, I know, but it is well worth the effort. You can solicit support from teachers and parents to help with writing. If you produce a newsletter monthly or quarterly, don't attempt to encompass in it all that has happened over that time period. Include short articles that highlight particular classrooms or particular staff members' accomplishments. Not only is it easier to write this way, but also there is a much better chance it will be read by parents if they do not have to comb through too much information. I always tried to include information about at least one staff member: what they were doing in the classroom, what workshop they had attended, or something about their latest endeavor outside the classroom.

Be innovative in your approach to parent communication. After exposure to a workshop on the Reggio Emilia curriculum, members of my staff developed storyboards to display in their classrooms and in the hallways. The storyboards included pictures of the children building structures in the block area, with captions explaining what skills the children were developing during their play. Since it is natural for parents to enjoy seeing pictures of their

Storyboard Presentation: The Value of Play

Note to Reader: Each section that follows should be accompanied by a photograph of the type of play being described.

Children need consistent, predictable, patterned, and frequent opportunities for play. Play is how children learn and process new information. Children are learning to think when they are: organizing ideas, setting tasks for themselves, talking, repeating what works, solving problems, challenging themselves, and trying new ideas.

Play requires the child to make choices and direct activities and often involves strategizing or planning to reach a goal.

Play helps children understand people and the importance of people's feelings.

Open-ended sensory play is a vital part of every child's cognitive, social, and emotional development. Every child that experiments with sensory materials experiences success. During sensory play experiences children learn: to see a task through to completion, to explore methods of movement, to play cooperatively with others, to use principles of math and science, and to problem-solve.

Creative movement, music, and dance expand a child's imagination. During play experiences with music and dance, children learn: about what their bodies can do; about rhythm, beats, and patterns; how music is a universal language that can bring people together.

The block area provides children with interesting construction materials precisely measured to give children many experiences with mathematics. Through play, children are confronted with many mental challenges having to do with measurement, equality, balance, shape, size, order, weight, gravity, stability, distance, spatial relationships, and physical properties. They learn how to share materials, to work together to build a construction, and to work out problems with others.

Dramatic play helps children experiment with and understand social roles and expectations while providing countless opportunities for acquiring social skills. During dramatic play experiences children learn: to use new words and word combinations in a risk-free environment, to create beyond the here and now, to take each other's needs into account and to appreciate different values and perspectives, and to exchange ideas and work together to solve problems.

(Compiled by Rob Mullen for his in-class presentation at Pacific Oaks College, Oakland, California.)

child engaged in activities they were not there to experience firsthand, the pictures draw the parents to the display. Even the busiest of parents has time to read an abbreviated description of their child's activity. Other teaching teams communicated with parents in monthly class newsletters, potluck suppers, or notebooks for each child in which there was a description of the child's participation in two or three activities a week.

Don't be afraid to brag about what you do; you should let parents know about the commitment and energy contributed by your teachers. Just as your employees like to know what is "going on" in the program, parents also need to be informed so they will really feel a part of your community.

Some programs also like to provide a formal mechanism for parents to communicate *to* the administration; i.e., to give voice to their needs. The large child care facility for which I was director had a parent committee with two representatives (each attending alternate months) from each classroom who met monthly with me. The committee gave parents an opportunity to plan and participate in the center's activities and have direct communication with me about their concerns. The committee also provided a way in which I could solicit parent help on community projects.

WORKING WITH MANAGEMENT AND WHY WE SHOULD CARE ABOUT OUR MANAGERS

Yes, I know. Our managers pay our salaries, and they can fire us. And, maybe, these two reasons are enough for us to pay attention to how we relate to our supervisors. But our managers can also make our lives pleasant or difficult. They can be supportive—trusting in our abilities and integrity, and giving us room to do our job. Or they can be so involved in what we do every day that we have no room to implement our own vision. For all of these reasons, we must care about the people who supervise us.

What Does Management Want from the Child Care Administrator?

I think this is a very good question for all of us to think about. Getting to know your supervisor(s) and what motivates him is essential to being successful in your role as the administrator.

- Does my supervisor only care about the bottom line?
- Is he interested in the quality of care provided in the program?
- Does she require that my program become an accredited center through the National Association for the Education of Young Children (NAEYC)?
- Is it important to her that she knows what is going on in the program on a regular basis? How much detail does she want?
- Is it important to him that I seek out his counsel and advice?

This may sound manipulative, and in a way it is. As the program administrator, you want to carry through on your vision and have enough resources to do so. The supervisor, or board, or owner, can be a huge asset to you. If they provide you with support rather than hinder your every move, your job will be that much easier and you can focus on the needs of your center. If your manager works *with* you rather than *against* you, you have a team with which to build a vision instead of being on your own.

Sometimes the people you work for don't want extensive or detailed information. I have worked for boards of directors (see next section) who wanted me to operate the center so that everyone in the community was satisfied. They did not want to hear the details of every complaint from employees or parents. They expected me to resolve all issues quietly. If you are working with this kind of board or manager, it is important to know because it requires a very different relationship between you and your supervisor.

How do you know what your supervisor wants from you? Often it is a matter of trial and error. You must listen closely to what management says to you and to what they *don't* say to you. Learn about the previous administrator: how was he successful or unsuccessful? I was once placed in the director position to succeed an administrator who had a very contentious relationship with the parent board of directors. It was very clear to me what kinds of behavior the board did not want to see again. You can try different frequencies of communication and different depths of reporting. Always respond promptly with the specific information being requested.

Working with a Board of Directors.   Getting to know your board members and what they want from you is important. If possible, it is helpful to meet regularly with the board president, or some other designated board member, to update them on what you've been doing and what has been happening with the staff. Trust develops through these regular meetings. This relationship building will go a long way toward helping you in the future if any difficult issues develop. It allows the board members to know what is going on and see that you are managing competently. And it allows you to control how, when, and what you share with the board.

Recruiting and training your board members are also important tasks. You should be proactive in finding board members who you feel will contribute positively to the mix of individuals already on the board. Think of how the personalities of the board members interact. What qualities, backgrounds, and skills are represented in the group? What qualities, backgrounds, or skills are missing from the present group?

Provide an opportunity for a board orientation annually in a location away from the center, where you review the board's role and its focus for the coming year. If possible, provide a speaker who can address the proper roles of board members. You want your board to focus on the bigger picture—long-range and strategic planning for your program—rather than on the day-to-day operations. The board should understand that fund-raising is one of their most important functions. Planning a fund-raising strategy is another important task of your board's orientation. There are excellent resources for training volunteer boards that you can access for little cost. See the listings following each chapter for books and Web sites on this subject.

Working with Parent Boards.   Over the years I have worked with a number of volunteer boards of directors. The most difficult group to work with, by far, is the volunteer board composed of parents in your program. Working for a board means that you have many bosses instead of just one; additionally, in the case of a parent board you are working for people who are your *clients*. These are people who have a great deal invested in how the center operates because their children are being served by it. Furthermore, most parents have little experience in early childhood education or in administering an early childhood program.

When you are recruiting parents to be on your board, talk with the parents with whom you have a good relationship and explore their viewpoints on the center's policies. The work you have already done in educating parents about your program and why you do what you do can help prepare them to become members of your board. I also recommend recruiting at least two community members for your board. These are individuals who have no current affiliation with your program, but who may contribute expertise, such as legal or fund development, to your organization. Having members from outside your program—who may serve many consecutive terms on your board—helps bring more of a balanced point of view to board decisions.

REFERENCES

Center for the Child Care Workforce. (1998). *Creating better child care jobs: Model work standards for teaching staff in center-based child care.* Washington, DC: Author.

Carver, J. (1997). *Boards that make a difference: A new design for leadership in nonprofit and public organizations* (2nd ed.). New York: Jossey-Bass.

Covey, S. R. (1989). *The seven habits of highly effective people.* New York: Simon and Schuster.

Glickman, C. (1981). *Developmental supervision: Alternative practices for helping teachers.* Alexandria, VA: Association for Supervision and Curriculum Development.

Goleman, D. (1995). *Emotional intelligence.* New York: Bantam Books.

Goleman, D. (2000, March–April). Leadership that gets good results. *Harvard Business Review,* 78.

Peters, T. J., & Waterman, R. H., Jr. (1982). *In search of excellence.* New York: Harper & Row.

Pointer, D. (2002). *The high-performance board.* New York: Jossey-Bass.

Tomal, D. (1992). Using the right personality style. *Supervision,* 53. Reprinted by permission of the National Research Bureau, 320 Valley Street, Burlington, Iowa 52601.

Webster's Collegiate Dictionary. (11th ed.). Springfield, MA: Merriam-Webster.

Whitebook, M., Sakai, L., Gerber, E., & Howes, C. (2001). *Then & now: Changes in child care staffing, 1994–2000.* Washington DC: Center for the Child Care Workforce, & Berkeley, CA: Institute of Industrial Relations.

CHAPTER 2

Enrollment, Staffing, and Tuition Fees

THE IMPORTANCE OF ENROLLMENT

The importance of the enrollment of children to the success of your organization cannot be overemphasized. By far, in almost all programs, revenue collected from the payment of tuition fees is the greatest portion of your income. It is the chief source of funding for all you do—the paying of wages to teachers, the payment of insurance premiums, rent payment, the purchase of food and supplies. If your enrollment is strong and tuition revenue steady, your program can withstand the ups and downs of the less important sources of income.

Enrollment is the one source of revenue over which you have the most control. You have little control over the rise and fall of funding from grants or other outside agencies. Fund-raising activities can be less successful than you had planned and you may find your program short thousands of dollars. Over the years, in all the programs I have managed, I have found that as long as our program was operating at near **capacity,** we were able to pay reasonable wages to staff, provide a good benefit package, fund capital improvements, and even build a surplus cash reserve. Only when we operated noticeably below capacity for a period of time did we find that we had to make cuts to operating expenses. When enrollment was low, even after cutting expenses, we all too often operated at a deficit.

When speaking about full enrollment in a program, I do not mean 100 percent enrollment. If your program offers any part-time schedules, it is virtually impossible to achieve 100 percent enrollment because it is not possible to fill every hour of every day with as many children as your license allows. Rather, I use the term "full enrollment" to mean being near capacity, which to me means having as many children as licensing (or accreditation) permits, most of the day, most days of the week. This is pretty vague, I know. Over a period of time, however, every administrator gets a feel for what "near capacity" means in her facility. You also get a feel for trade-offs: how under enrollment in one age group can be

Enrollment is the key to financial stability in any size child care program.

partially offset by capacity enrollment in another age group. Or, how low enrollment may need to be offset by a temporary reduction in staff hours.

Relationship to Staffing

On the other side of the financial equation from tuition revenue, of course, is what you spend. And under "spending," the largest category is always staff wages and benefits. It is important to keep in mind that you want to monitor staffing costs continually, even when you have full enrollment. You should always be thinking in terms of *staffing to enrollment*, not staffing to your capacity. A high level of enrollment, that is, at capacity, or near capacity, allows you to maintain a full staffing level. If you are not enrolled close to your capacity, you have to consider having fewer teaching hours in your program. A full level of staffing can remain for a period of time when enrollment falls. You don't want to lay off teachers or cut the hours of teachers you will need again when enrollment picks up. Yet, on the other hand, you cannot continue to pay a full level of staff if your enrollment remains low, or if you forecast it will continue to be below capacity for longer than four to six weeks. We will explore this subject in much more detail in Chapter 3.

DETERMINING YOUR CAPACITY

The first step in determining what your enrollment can be is to determine how many children you are legally allowed to have in your program. This is your program's capacity. Depending on the state in which you are located, there are specific licensing regulations to which you must conform.

State Licensing and NAEYC Accreditation Guidelines

The licensing regulations in your state delineate the legal child-to-teacher ratios for both privately and publicly licensed child care programs. The state also determines the usable interior space and outdoor space required for each child. (The National Resource Center for Health and Safety in Child Care maintains a useful Web site—<http://www.nrc. uchsc.edu>—which lists all child care licensing regulations by state.) Using these regulations, an administrator can determine the *maximum* size group that can be enrolled in any classroom, and can also determine the *minimum* number of teaching staff required. In Figure 2–1, the group size and number of teachers are determined for three classrooms at the Felton Family Preschool, where the state requires 35 square feet inside and 75 square feet outside for each child.

If your program is accredited by NAEYC (see "Useful Web Sites," Appendix C), or follows other guidelines that are more restrictive than your state's licensing regulations, you may define your capacity as less than the maximum number of children allowed. In Figure 2–1, the licensed capacity for toddlers (18–30 months) is 16 children based on the inside and outside space available. The NAEYC guideline for group size for this age is a minimum of 6 up to a maximum of 14 children. The Felton Family Preschool has chosen to limit their group size in this age group to 15 regularly attending children even though they have space for up to 16 children. This number of children will allow them to staff the room with three teachers and maintain a ratio of 1 to 5. In California, a group of children where some are younger than two years and some are older than two years is a special category called a "toddler component." By special application, these age groups can be combined if the teacher-to-child ratio is 1 to 6 or better. In a similar way, the group sizes and teacher-to-child ratios are determined for the other two classrooms in the Felton Family Preschool.

In another example, if your preschool classroom has 900 square feet of usable indoor space and 2,300 square feet of outdoor space, you would be limited to enrolling 25 children

Felton Family Preschool
Group Size Determination

Classroom	Inside Square Feet	Licensed Capacity	Outside Square Feet	Licensed Capacity	Group Size NAEYC	Group Size Felton Family	Teacher/Child Ratio
18–30 Months	650	18.57	1200	16.00	6-14	15	1/5
30–42 Months	700	20.00	1250	16.67	12-14	16	1/8
42 Months +	725	20.71	1650.00	22.00	14-20	20	1/10

FIGURE 2–1 Felton Family Preschool Group Size Determination

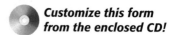
Customize this form from the enclosed CD!

in that space (900 divided by 35 square feet = 25.7 children and 2,300 divided by 75 = 30.7 children). However, if you are also working toward accreditation with NAEYC, you might decide to limit your preschool group to only 20 children. That means that *at any one time* there are a maximum of 20 children attending, not that you have enrolled only 20 children. Depending on how many children attend only part-time, say three days a week, or only mornings, you may have a total of 25 or 27 children enrolled in the class.

Flexibility: Responding to Demand

In this classroom of 20 preschoolers described in the preceding paragraph, we can also allow for the attendance going over 20, since state *licensed* capacity (what licensing regulations allow) is 25 in the classroom. NAEYC recommends a teacher-to-child ratio for this age group of 1 to 10. Since state licensing requires a minimum ratio of 1 to 12 for a private program for this age, two teachers in the classroom can legally cover up to 24 children at any one time.

Such a situation might occur, for example, in response to lower demand in the toddler classroom. If your toddler room enrollment is low by one or two children, and you do not anticipate being able to fill those spaces in the near term, you want to be flexible enough to add children in classes where you have the demand. In this way, you are maintaining the center's enrollment at the highest level possible. As children become developmentally ready to move into an older group, you also want your program to have the flexibility to accommodate them without a long delay. You cannot *keep* openings in classes so that there is always room for one or two children to move up. But you can be aware of where you can bend a little in order to respond to these needs and to the changing needs of your families.

Flexibility also means being able to accommodate the temporary needs of one of your families when they want their child to attend four days instead of only three for the next two weeks while the child's mother is traveling. Even though having this child on the extra day will increase your count to 21, you are still legally compliant, and you have also been able to help out one of your currently enrolled families. The extra income for that child attending an extra day will help your program. Or, perhaps, you can accommodate a child that has already graduated from your program when he needs summer care after completing kindergarten, even though this will mean that your count in the preschool class is 22 on two days a week.

✓Hint

Flexibility is the key to maintaining your enrollment near capacity.

MAINTAINING HIGH ENROLLMENT

The key to the financial stability of any child care program is maintaining enrollment at or near capacity. You must always keep this in mind when you are moving children into an older classroom and creating spaces in the younger-age room and when you are losing children who are graduating to kindergarten. There are several things you can be doing in order to keep ahead of this challenging aspect of running your program.

Know Your Market

Knowing your market is a maxim for any business. What does it mean? For child care administrators, it means knowing the child care needs of your current families as well as those of other families in your community who are potential clients of your program. It means knowing a little about the general state of the economy and how economic ups and downs are affecting your families.

For many years, the program I directed never had to worry about its "market" or demand for its services. We had long waiting lists for all of our classes. For our two infant classrooms, we had lists of over 100 families. But then the dot-com bust occurred in the Silicon Valley, and over a period of months the economy in California faltered, companies were reducing spending, employees were losing their jobs, and the state government and public agencies were operating with large budget deficits. Over the course of a year I watched our waiting lists grow smaller. The families on our waiting lists whom we called to offer openings in our program, no longer wanted care. We were calling through pages of names, and not one of the families wanted to enroll their child at the time of our call. Families already enrolled in our program began asking more frequently to change their child's schedule to fewer days and/or fewer hours. Parents were losing their jobs and no longer needed the care, or no longer needed full-time care. Families were moving out of the San Francisco Bay area because there were no jobs, but the cost of living (mainly housing costs) continued to be high. We no longer had the luxury of knowing there would always be families lined up to enter our program. We had to understand the economy, and understand the changing needs of the families within our community. For the first time in many years, we had to work to keep our center enrolled.

It is not difficult to learn enough about your community to understand the changing needs of your clients. One good way is talking to the parents in your program, learning their personal stories. The employees of your organization who live in the community will have stories of their own about a husband's job loss, or downsizing in their sister's company. As parents request schedule changes, talk with them about their changing requirements for child care. You could even conduct a short parent survey to determine current and future needs of the families in your program, such as the survey depicted in Figure 2–2. You may want to make this kind of survey a regular practice. The information you gather can be very helpful, especially if you anticipate a lot of changes over the summer when families take vacations and five-year-olds exit the program. The results of such an annual survey can help you decide whether to start a special summertime program for five-year-olds.

Reading the headline news stories and the business section of your newspaper will help you understand the changes that are occurring in your community. This is something you can be doing whether your center is fully enrolled or not. Knowing about the economic climate and predictions for the future helps you anticipate when changes in demand for your services may occur.

Staying Ahead of Falling Enrollment

Keeping a child care program fully enrolled at all times is a full-time job. That means there should ideally be someone on your staff whose job is devoted to keeping children enrolled

Parent Survey

In order to plan for your child's care over the next year, it is essential that we know your vacation plans over the summer and your requirements for care in the fall. For each child needing care, please complete a separate form, and return it to the office by Friday, March 28. Thank you for your help.

Name of child: Birth date:

Vacation dates this summer?

Summer schedule desired: (check one)

☐ 5 full days   ☐ 5 mornings (7:30–12:30)

☐ 3 full days   ☐ 5 afternoons (1:00–6:00)

Which days? _____

Fall schedule desired: (check one)

☐ 5 full days   ☐ 5 mornings (7:30–12:30)

☐ 3 full days   ☐ 5 afternoons (1:00–6:00)

Which days? _____

Parent signature: Date:

FIGURE 2–2 Parent Survey

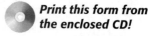

Print this form from the enclosed CD!

✓ Hint

Think about your enrollment all the time and try to anticipate what enrollment will look like in the future.

in all classes. Large programs have the luxury of designating one full-time employee for this task, who does *nothing but* enrollment. In smaller or new programs, you, as the administrator, may be doing everything, including enrollment of families. Whoever is responsible for this task should understand it is a vital one for the organization. You have to think about enrollment all the time as the administrator, including reading your crystal ball to see what next week, next month, and next year look like.

Your Enrolled Families.   The first place to look for information about future enrollment is the families currently enrolled in your program. By speaking with parents, you may be able to understand their current and future child care needs. As mentioned above, written surveys can help too. Every spring, our center asked parents to complete a survey about their summer vacation plans. We also asked them what schedule they wanted to reserve for their child for the fall. This information was then compiled and combined with information about which children would be moving up into older age groups over the next several months. This process enabled us to anticipate where and when we would need space for

! TIP

Staying in touch with
your enrolled families
is one of the best
ways to learn about
and anticipate your
community's changing
needs for child care.

children, and what spaces would be created in the classrooms children were leaving. We could anticipate part-time spaces that might develop when families were on vacation. A spring survey also helped us look at the configuration of classes for the next academic term, to plan staffing and enrollment of new families into the program.

Notice of children exiting is obviously important for planning purposes too. Most programs have a policy that requires families to give notice to the administration that they will be leaving. Typically, a 2-week or 30-day notice is required, which is the minimum amount of time you will need to plan for filling that space.

Waiting Lists.   Your other best source of information for planning future enrollment is your waiting list. Many programs use some form of waiting list. Even if you run a small family child care program, having a list of "interested" families is essential to being able to plan for the future, even if all you have is a handwritten list you have created as calls come in to your home.

For other than family child care, I recommend charging a small fee for families wanting to be on a waiting list. There is some cost to you in administrative time in getting and keeping the information on that family in a database. And the fee also helps to ensure the families who get on your list are serious about wanting to enroll in your program. It is a one-time, nonrefundable fee that will keep the family on the list until they are offered a space in your program, or until they let you know they no longer want care.

A waiting list that grows endlessly and is never maintained, however, is not a very reliable tool for planning. The longer the list is, the more this is true, and the harder it is to find time to do the maintenance. At the very least, annual maintenance of waiting lists should be done. Calling each family on the list to review their current needs and make updates to their record in the database can be done if your waiting list is not extensive. I have even hired a part-time student during the summer to do only this task. With longer lists it is easier and less costly to mail letters with a return postcard enclosed. The letter asks the same questions you would ask in a phone call, e.g., whether the family wants to remain on the waiting list, and if so, to complete the postcard with

- current address and phone number
- children's names and birth dates for those needing child care
- child care schedules required
- start date needed for child care

If the family wants to remain on your list, then it is up to them to return the card to you by a specified date. As cards come back in, you can update each record on your waiting list. Families who do not return the cards, or who indicate they no longer need care, are taken off your list.

Whenever possible it is even better to maintain close contact with the families at or near the top of the waiting list. This helps you know which families are ready to enroll as soon as an opening occurs. If you anticipate openings, it is okay to call the top families to give them notification that an opening is about to occur and when you expect it will be available. An incoming family may need time to make plans for their child's enrollment.

DETERMINING YOUR FEE STRUCTURE

One of the most difficult aspects of setting up and/or maintaining the business of a child care organization is determining the structure of tuition fees you are going to charge. There is no formula. There is no "best" method. Often it comes down to trial and error to see what works in your own particular circumstances. But there are some guidelines I can recommend.

Market Rate Comparison

The first place to begin is to look at what other programs in your community are charging. Your program may be qualitatively different, may serve a larger span of age groups, may be open longer hours, or may have any number of distinguishing qualities, but a market survey is always a good place to start. Even if you feel your services are superior to anything else in the community, you can find there will be only limited demand if you price your services too far above the competition.

Information about your competitors can come from surveys that have been done in your area by an outside agency. Your local resource and referral agency may compile countywide statistics on what child care programs cost for different levels of care. I have done surveys myself by spending a couple of hours on the telephone calling four or five facilities in my neighborhood. I tell them who I am and why I am calling, and ask for their fee information. This is always something I am more than willing to share with other administrators. They have the same difficulty in setting their fees as I do. I encourage you to network with other child care programs in your community whether in a formal organization or informally through personal contact. The sharing of information can only help you do your job better, and, at the very least, remind you that you are not alone out there struggling to do your job.

Full Cost of Care and Hourly Rate

In 1990, NAEYC published *Reaching the Full Cost of Quality in Early Childhood Programs* (Willer). This was a pioneering publication in that for the first time ever, early childhood educators were quantifying how much it really costs to provide a high level of care in early childhood and exploring the devastating economic impacts of failing to reach quality in programs for young children. Equally important, I think, is Chapter 6 in which Barbara Willer, at that time the Public Affairs Director of NAEYC, demonstrates how to measure the **full cost of care** in your own program. Determining the full cost of care in your program tells you what it currently costs you to provide care for children. It gives you other target figures, along with market comparison rates, on which to base your fee structure.

Following is a description of a method, based on the chapter 6 by Barbara Willer, that can be used to determine your current cost of care. You will be using your current operating cost figures to develop the cost of care in your program. If you are just starting a program, you first have to determine your staffing requirements and staff salaries as well as your other costs before you can determine what the full cost of care is in your program. (Chapter 4 provides a full description of the budget-building process.) We'll take a look here at determining the staffing needs of your child care program.

Teachers and Staffing Ratios.   The first step in assessing your organization's need for staff, whether you are just opening a facility or are continuing in an ongoing program, is to determine how many staff you need to run your classrooms. You will be looking at the state regulations for minimum staff-to-child ratios. In California, the licensing ratio for children under two years of age is 1 to 4, and over two years of age is 1 to 12 in private programs. In the state of Vermont, the required ratios are 1 to 4 for children up to two years of age, 1 to 5 for children ages two years up to three years, and 1 to 10 for children three years through kindergarten (National Resource Center for Health and Safety in Child Care database). These ratios dictate the *minimum* numbers of teachers required to meet licensing regulations and they differ state by state. They define the floor below which your staffing cannot go. Other guidelines may provide stricter ratios with which you and your program may want to comply. As administrator, you must also consider coverage for breaks and lunches, for some overlap of staff between shifts, and possibly for time for teachers to prepare the classroom at the beginning of the day and clean up the room at the close of the day when children are not present.

Felton Family Preschool

Staffing Pattern

TODDLER ROOM - RATIO 1/5 Number of Children Attending Each Hour

Hrs/Wk	Employee name	7:30	8:30	9:30	10:30	11:30	12:30	1:30	2:30	3:30	4:30	5:30	6:00
		3	10	15	15	15	15	15	15	15	15/12	8	0
40	Latifa	1	1	1	1	1	1	1	1	1/			
30	Sheena	/1	1	1	1	1	1	1					
40	Carol		/1	1	1	1	1	1	1	1	1		
32.5	Jean-Claude				/1	1	1	1	1	1	1	1	
17.5	Marta									1	1	1	1
	Number of Teachers Present Each Hour												
		1/2	2/3	3	3/4	4	4	4	4	4/3	3	2	

Total Staff Hours per Week   160

Staffing Pattern - with Prep Time and Breaks

Number of Children Attending Each Hour

Hrs/Wk	Employee name	7:00	7:30	8:30	9:30	10:30	11:30	12:30	1:30	2:30	3:30	4:30	5:30	6:00
		0	3	10	15	15	15	15	15	15	15	15/12	8	0
40	Latifa	1	1	1	1	1	1	1	1	1				
30	Sheena		/1	1	1	1	1	1	1	1				
40	Carol			/1	1	1	1	1	1	1	1	1		
35	Jean-Claude					1	1	1	1	1	1	1	1	
20	Marta										1	1	1	1
	Number of Teachers Present Each Hour													
		1	1/2	2/3	3	4	4	4	4	4	3	3	2	0

Total Staff Hours per Week   165

** A "/" in the column indicates when a staff member arrives half-way through the hour.
For example, in the staffing pattern above, Carol's shift starts at 8:00 A.M.

FIGURE 2–3 Felton Family Preschool Staffing Pattern

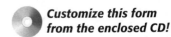

Customize this form from the enclosed CD!

! TIP

Although a staffing pattern chart helps you figure out the *minimum* staffing requirements for each classroom, familiarity with what is happening in each room at all times of the day is necessary in order to determine the level of staffing to support *quality* care.

A useful tool for helping you figure out the staffing for a classroom is a worksheet where you display the shifts of the teachers in each classroom for all hours of the day. This worksheet can be constructed with paper and pencil, or can be developed in a computer spreadsheet. Figure 2–3 is an illustration of such a worksheet. The first pattern describes the minimum teaching schedules required for the Felton Preschool's toddler room, maintaining a ratio of 1/5 through morning and afternoon breaks and the midday period when teachers will be taking lunch breaks. The second pattern on the page shows schedules for the same class in which changes have been made to allow for teacher prep time before the center opens and cleanup time after the center closes. The advantage of using the computer model is, of course, that you can instantly display changes you make to teacher schedules, ratios, breaks, etc. The worksheets can be used again and again for changes in personnel and changes in classroom configuration. For smaller programs with fewer staff and fewer classrooms, a hand-drawn model is perfectly adequate.

	Employee	Current Wage Rate	Hours/Wk	Annual Salary	
Felton Family Preschool					
Staff Salaries					
Toddler Staff					
	Latifa	$11.00	40	$22,880	
	Sheena	$9.50	30	$14,820	
	Carol	$8.00	40	$16,640	
	Jean-Claude	$10.50	35	$19,110	
	Marta	$10.00	20	$10,400	
				$83,850	
Young Preschool Staff					
	Francis	$9.00	40	$18,720	
	Georgia	$9.00	30	$14,040	
	Janisha	$11.00	30	$17,160	
	Juan	$11.00	40	$22,880	
				$72,800	
Pre-K Staff					
	Dtr/Teacher	$12.00	10	$6,240	
	Isabel	$10.00	40	$20,800	
	Jodie	$9.75	35	$17,745	
	Linda	$8.00	40	$16,640	
				$61,425	
	Dtr/Teacher	$12.00	30	$18,720	
	Substitutes			$8,205	
	TOTAL SALARIES			$245,000	
	TOTAL SALARIES LESS SUBS			$236,795	

FIGURE 2–4 Felton Family Preschool Staff Salaries

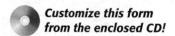

Customize this form from the enclosed CD!

When you have determined both the minimum staffing you need to run your program and the desired number of staff to produce the highest quality of care, you can transfer this information to a staff salary spreadsheet as in Figure 2–4. By multiplying a teacher's hourly wage rate times the number of hours she works each week you can compute each teacher's salary per week.

$11.00 per hour times 40 hours per week = $440/week.

If she works twelve months, which is 52 weeks, of the year, then her annual salary is

$440 times 52 weeks = $22,880 per year.

Other Staff. For the Felton Family Preschool, there is only one other regular staff member in addition to the teaching staff—the director, who also works in the preschool room

10 hours per week. The director would like to be able to hire an assistant someday, but budget restrictions currently make this impossible.

Most programs can benefit from having more than one person in the office. This permits better coverage of phones and walk-in business, whether it is parents, teachers, or potential clients. For security purposes, it is also important to have someone located within view of the front door to observe who enters the building. Moreover, a second office employee allows for the distribution of financial jobs so that the proper checks and balances can occur. For example, the individual who produces the bills for families should never be the same person who receives the payments. (See Chapter 6.)

Larger programs may have an assistant director, a bookkeeper, program supervisors, or even a human resources manager. In the 120-family program that I managed, our administrative team consisted of a staffing and enrollment coordinator, a business manager, an infant/toddler program coordinator, a preschool program coordinator, and a mentor teacher. The two program coordinators spent half their time in the classroom, and each supervised a staff of about 17 teachers and teaching assistants. The business manager handled all the financial affairs and the staffing coordinator enrolled new families and managed the time-off schedules of teachers and the use of substitutes. The mentor teacher worked individually with staff, and conducted new staff orientation workshops and parent education workshops.

Determining Full Current Cost of Care.   The first piece in determining the full cost of care in your program is to calculate the total of all administrative costs of your center. Annual administrative, or **overhead,** costs such as rent, insurance, *administrative* salaries, benefits, and taxes, are totaled, then divided by the total number of children in your facility. This gives you the **cost per child** per year for administration expenses. To this figure, you must add the cost of salaries, benefits, and taxes for the *teachers* who work in *each age group,* and divide this total by the number of children in that age group at your center. Figures 2–5 and 2–6 illustrate how to compute the full cost of care for the Felton Family Preschool.

Figure 2–5 is the same as Figure 2–4 ("Staff Salaries") with Columns F and G, and Rows 36 and 37 added. Rather than add up the exact cost of each employee's benefits, I have used a method based on percentages. Total staff benefits are shown in Row 37, and come from the school's budget. In Column F, I calculated the percent that a classroom's teacher salaries are of the total *benefited* salaries (i.e., don't count the salaries of substitutes since they do not receive insurance or educational benefits). Since total salaries in the young preschool class are 31 percent of the total benefited salaries ($72,800 divided by $236,795), I charged 31 percent, or $9,185 ($29,875 times .31), of the total dollar value of the annual benefits ($29,875) to the young preschool room. In a similar way, the spreadsheet calculated the dollar value of benefits for each classroom and for the director.

This is somewhat of a simplification over adding in the exact cost of benefits for each employee. Using a percentage method will not change the outcome in a significant way and makes the computation quite a bit easier. These salary and benefit figures are transferred from Figure 2–5 to Figure 2–6 under either administrative costs (for the director's salary and benefits) or classroom expense.

The classroom salaries and benefits are transferred to the bottom of Figure 2–6 (Columns C and F, Rows 41 through 43). Payroll tax and worker's compensation insurance for each classroom are computed in Columns D and E by the following formulas:

Salary times 9% = payroll tax, or

$83,850 times .09 = $7,546

$72,800 times .09 = $6,552

$61,425 times .09 = $5,528

Staff Salaries & Benefits

Total Toddler Staff

Employee	Current Wage Rate	Hours/Wk	Annual Salary	% of Total Less Subs	Benefit Amount
Latifa	$11.00	40	$22,880		
Sheena	$9.50	30	$14,820		
Carol	$8.00	40	$16,640		
Jean-Claude	$10.50	35	$19,110		
Marta	$10.00	20	$10,400		
			$83,850	35%	$10,578

Total Young Preschool

Francis	$9.00	40	$18,720		
Georgia	$9.00	30	$14,040		
Janisha	$11.00	30	$17,160		
Juan	$11.00	40	$22,880		
			$72,800	31%	$9,185

Total Pre-K Staff

Dtr/Teacher	$12.00	10	$6,240		
Isabel	$10.00	40	$20,800		
Jodie	$9.75	35	$17,745		
Linda	$8.00	40	$16,640		
			$61,425	26%	$7,750

Dtr/Teacher	$12.00	30	$18,720	8%	$2,362
Substitutes			$8,205		

	TOTAL SALARIES		$245,000		

	TOTAL SALARIES LESS SUBS		$236,795	100%	

Benefits:	Health Ins.	Dental Ins.	Educ. Allow	Total	
	25,000	4,000	875	$29,875	

FIGURE 2–5 Felton Family Preschool Staff Salaries and Benefits

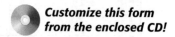

Customize this form from the enclosed CD!

Salary, divided by 100, times $5 = worker's comp insurance (worker's compensation insurance is usually charged as a dollar rate per $100 of payroll cost), or

$83,850 divided by 100 times $5.00 = $4,192

$72,800 divided by 100 times $5.00 = $3,640

$61,425 divided by 100 times $5.00 = $3,071.

In the center of Figure 2–6 under the heading "Annual Exp/Admin Costs," all the administrative (or overhead) costs are accumulated. As part of administrative costs I have added 75 percent of the teacher/director's salary (since she spends 10 hours a week in the preschool classroom, and 30 hours a week on her director duties), all the substitute

Felton Family Preschool
Computing the Full Cost of Care

	Classroom	Number of Children	Admin Cost per Child	Classroom Cost per Child	Annual Total Cost per Child	Monthly Total Cost per Child
18–30 Months		15	1,406	7,078	8,484	707
30–42 Months		16	1,406	5,761	7,168	597
42 Months +		20	1,406	3,889	5,295	441
Total Enrolled		51				

	Annual Exp Admin Costs
Dtr & Sub Salaries	26,925
Director Benefits	2,362
Payroll Tax	2,423
Worker's Comp	1,346
Rent	4,800
Janitor	6,000
Insurance	5,175
Supplies	20,000
Utilities	2,700
Capital Improv.	0
Total Admin Costs	71,732
Admin Cost/Child	1,406

Classroom Expense

	Salaries	Payroll Tax	Worker's Comp	Benefits	Total
Toddlers	83,850	7,546	4,192	10,579	106,168
Young PS	72,800	6,552	3,640	9,185	92,177
Preschool	61,425	5,528	3,071	7,750	77,774
Total Sal & Ben.	274,876				

FIGURE 2–6 Felton Family Preschool Computing the Full Cost of Care

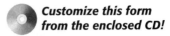

Customize this form from the enclosed CD!

salary costs, payroll taxes that are 9 percent of these salaries, and the percentage of staff benefits attributed to the director that was computed in Figure 2–5.

The total annual administrative costs for the school are $71,732. Since we have defined the capacity of the program as 51 children, the administrative cost per child is

$71,732 divided by 51, or $1,406.

The administrative cost per child is the *same* across all programs in the Felton School and is transferred to the top of the worksheet in Figure 2–6 in Column D, Rows 12, 15, and 18.

The second part of the computation requires adding the teacher salaries, payroll taxes, worker's compensation insurance, and benefits for each classroom. In column E of Figure 2–6, the total of the expenses for each classroom has been divided by the number of children in the class to determine the classroom cost per child. For example, dividing the total for the preschool room, $77,774 (Column G, Row 43), by the number of children in preschool (20) yields a figure of $3,889 as the classroom cost per child.

Preschool cost per child $3,889.

To this figure is added the administrative cost per child

Admin. cost per child $1,406,

to determine the full cost of care per child, as follows:

Total cost/child in preschool = $5,295 per year
OR $441 per month.

This number represents the full monthly cost of providing care for each child in the preschool program. When putting together a fee structure, this cost represents *the floor below which you do not want to set your fees*.

In a similar manner, the full cost of care in the other two programs is calculated. They can be used as additional target points for your fee structure. These figures are costs for the full-time child since you have used your full-time enrollment capacity to compute these costs.

You can derive the hourly costs of care in the age groups in your program from these monthly cost figures. In preschool, if a full-time child attends an average of 20 days per month, and is in school for approximately 9 hours per day, she attends 180 hours per month (9 times 20). The hourly cost of her care is

$441 divided by 180 hours per month, or $2.45 per hour.

For a child in the toddler program, the computation would be

$707 divided by 180 hours per month, or $3.93 per hour.

The Full Cost of Quality Care

A third set of data points for you to calculate to help in structuring your tuition fees, is what is called the **full cost of *quality* care.** This is the full cost of providing care to the children in your program if you are spending the money to create a community that is able to

> "Foster *good relationships between children and adults* by limiting group sizes and the number of children per adult, promoting continuity for children, and enhancing staff-parent relationships";
> "Ensure that educational personnel have qualifications reflecting the *specialized preparation and knowledge* needed to work effectively with young children and their families";
> "Provide *adequate compensation* (salaries and benefits) to attract and retain qualified staff"; and
> "Establish an *environment that enhances children's ability to learn* in a safe and stimulating setting and *provides good working conditions* for adults." (Willer, p. 2)

If we assume the preschool in our example is now providing all the elements of *quality* care as defined above except for adequate salaries for staff, then to compute the *full cost of quality care,* we must make the same computation as in the last section, but use the *target*

Felton Family Preschool
Target Salaries & Benefits

Total Toddler Staff

Employee	Target Wage Rate	Hours/Wk	Annual Salary	% of Total Less Subs	Benefit Amount
Latifa	$15.75	40	$32,760		
Sheena	$13.00	30	$20,280		
Carol	$11.00	40	$22,880		
Jean-Claude	$15.00	35	$27,300		
Marta	$14.00	20	$14,560		
			$117,780	36%	$10,639

Total Young Preschool

Employee	Target Wage Rate	Hours/Wk	Annual Salary	% of Total Less Subs	Benefit Amount
Francis	$13.00	40	$27,040		
Georgia	$13.00	30	$20,280		
Janisha	$15.00	30	$23,400		
Juan	$15.00	40	$31,200		
			$101,920	31%	$9,207

Total Pre-K Staff

Employee	Target Wage Rate	Hours/Wk	Annual Salary	% of Total Less Subs	Benefit Amount
Dtr/Teacher	$17.00	10	$8,840		
Isabel	$14.00	40	$29,120		
Jodie	$13.00	35	$23,660		
Linda	$11.00	40	$22,880		
			$84,500	26%	$7,633
Dtr/Teacher	$17.00	30	$26,520	8%	$2,396
Substitutes			$15,000		
	TOTAL SALARIES		$345,720		
	TOTAL SALARIES LESS SUBS		$330,720	100%	

Benefits:	Health Ins.	Dental Ins.	Educ. Allow	Total	
	25,000	4,000	875	$29,875	

FIGURE 2–7 Felton Family Preschool Target Salaries and Benefits

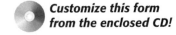

Customize this form from the enclosed CD!

salaries for our staff instead of their current salaries. This is what has been done in Figures 2–7 and 2–8.

Staff wages in Column C of Figure 2–7 have been modified to reflect a **living wage** in this preschool's community. A living wage is what is required for an individual or family to live in a particular community; i.e., be able to afford housing, food, and clothing. In 2002, a minimum hourly wage of $11.00 with benefits was established as the living wage in the county of Santa Cruz, California. All employees of the preschool are thus targeted to earn a minimum of $11.00 per hour. Higher salaries are based on an employee's education and experience. The director of the preschool is now targeted to earn slightly more than $35,000 per year.

Based on these target salaries, a new cost of care computation is completed in Figure 2–8. As salaries increase, there is a corresponding increase in payroll taxes and worker's

Felton Family Preschool
Computing the Full Cost of Quality Care
Using Target Salaries

Classroom	Number of Children	Admin Cost per Child	Classroom Cost per Child	Annual Total Cost per Child	Monthly Total Cost per Child
18–30 Months	15	1,733	9,661	11,394	949
30–42 Months	16	1,733	7,837	9,571	798
42 Months +	20	1,733	5,198	6,932	578
Total Enrolled	51				

	Annual Exp Budget
Dtr & Sub Salaries	41,520
Director Benefits	2,396
Payroll Tax	3,737
Worker's Comp	2,076
Rent	4,800
Janitor	6,000
Insurance	5,175
Supplies	20,000
Utilities	2,700
Capital Improv.	0
Total Admin Costs	88,404
Admin Cost/Child	1,733

Classroom Expense

	Salaries	Payroll Tax	Worker's Comp	Benefits	Total
Toddlers	117,780	10,600	5,889	10,639	144,908
Young PS	101,920	9,173	5,096	9,207	125,396
Preschool	84,500	7,605	4,225	7,633	103,963
Total Sal & Ben.	274,876				

FIGURE 2–8 Felton Family Preschool Computing the Full Cost of Quality Care

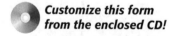

Customize this form from the enclosed CD!

compensation insurance. These increases are reflected in the administrative and classroom costs for the center. As you can see by comparing the figures in Column G in Figure 2–8 (monthly cost of *quality* care) to the figures in column G in Figure 2–9 (monthly cost of *current* care), the full cost of care *has risen by 31 percent to 34 percent* for each program. These higher cost figures determine the direction in which we hope to move our program and they enter into our determination of current tuition rates.

The figures showing the full cost of quality care also help us to talk to parents and community members about the struggle between affordability and quality in our early childhood programs. "It is imperative to know the full cost of providing a quality service so that various segments of society—employers, foundations, service organizations, government—can then determine how they can support these costs" (Willer, p. 55).

Felton Family Preschool
Computing the Full Cost of Care

	Classroom	Number of Children	Admin Cost per Child	Classroom Cost per Child	Annual Total Cost per Child	Monthly Total Cost per Child
18–30 Months		15	1,406	7,078	8,484	707
30–42 Months		16	1,406	5,761	7,168	597
42 Months +		20	1,406	3,889	5,295	441
Total Enrolled		51				

	Annual Exp Admin Costs
Dtr & Sub Salaries	26,925
Director Benefits	2,362
Payroll Tax	2,423
Worker's Comp	1,346
Rent	4,800
Janitor	6,000
Insurance	5,175
Supplies	20,000
Utilities	2,700
Capital Improv.	0
Total Admin Costs	71,732
Admin Cost/Child	1,406

Classroom Expense

	Salaries	Payroll Tax	Worker's Comp	Benefits	Total
Toddlers	83,850	7,546	4,192	10,579	106,168
Young PS	72,800	6,552	3,640	9,185	92,177
Preschool	61,425	5,528	3,071	7,750	77,774
Total Sal & Ben.	274,876				

FIGURE 2–9 Felton Family Preschool Computing the Full Cost of Care

Part-Time Care versus Full-Time Care

In many ways, full-time care is the easiest to provide. Full-time children usually become accustomed to the routine of the program and to their caregivers more quickly than do part-time children. Full-time care is also the "standard" kind of child care that is requested by working parents. Any kind of part-time care is then considered not standard. Part-time care is sometimes harder to provide as children are making transitions into the program or from the program during the course of the day or the week. Schedules in which children attend half days for less than five days a week often create "holes" in the attendance that you can never fill with other children.

Felton Family Preschool

Determination of Fee Structure

Age of Child	Market Rate School A	Market Rate School B	Market Rate School C	Market Rate School D	Current Cost per Child	Full Quality Cost per Child	Felton Preschool
18–30 Months							
Full-time rates	725	850	925	660	707	949	825
Half-time rates	400	500	500	375			500
30–42 Months							
Full-time rates	575	750	750	560	597	798	700
Half-time rates	350	450	450	400			425
42 Months +							
Full-time rates	475	650	575	460	441	578	525
Half-time rates	300	400	325	300			350

		Monthly Tuition			Monthly Tuition
18–30 Months	full-time	825			
	full-time:reduced rate	635			
	half-time	500			
	half-time:reduced rate	340			
	3 days/week	600			
	3-day:reduced rate	425			
30–42 Months	full-time	700	**42 Months +** full-time		525
	full-time:reduced rate	480	full-time:reduced rate		400
	half-time	425	half-time		350
	half-time:reduced rate	300	half-time:reduced rate		230
	3 days/week	550	3 days/week		425
	3-day:reduced rate	400	3-day:reduced rate		300

FIGURE 2–10 Felton Family Preschool Determination of Fee Structure

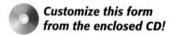

Customize this form from the enclosed CD!

For these reasons, I recommend charging a premium for any part-time schedule in your program. In other words, for a child attending half-time, set a fee that is slightly more than one-half the full-time rate, and for a child attending three days a week, slightly more than three-fifths of the full-time rate. Parents usually expect to pay slightly more for a schedule that exactly fits their needs rather than having to pay for a full-time schedule when they are not using the full number of hours for their child.

Creating the Fee Structure

Now that we have several data points from which to work, we can begin to determine what our tuition fee structure will look like. The final determination will have to wait until we assemble our full budget (see Chapter 4) and balance the revenue and expense sides of our financial picture. We start with a display of all the target data points we have collected so far (see Figure 2–10).

The first four data columns list the full-time and half-time fees for the age groups listed from the schools in our survey. Columns G and H list the figures for current cost of care (from Figure 2–9) and full quality cost of care (Figure 2–8). We know the following:

- We want to set our full-time fees to cover completely the current cost of care per child.
- We don't want to charge the lowest fees in the community.
- We probably don't want to charge the highest fees in the community, although it is not necessarily wrong to do so.

Because the Felton Family Preschool offers reduced-rate tuition fees to some families, we may need to charge *more* than current costs to the families paying full fees. In essence, the full-fare families are subsidizing the reduced-rate families unless we are able to obtain outside funding to do this.

An initial set of rates for families paying full fees is listed in Column I. Each rate is more than the current cost of care, less than or equal to the highest fees charged by schools in our community, and higher than the lowest fees charged. We have fitted our fees near the top rates in the community because we feel that the quality of care we provide supports charging more than some of the other programs.

The monthly tuition structure for all part-time and full-time rates, for full fees and reduced-rate fees, is shown in the lower section of Figure 2–10. I'd like to be able to tell you the "formulas" for arriving at these numbers. But, quite honestly, I use "guesstimation" for determining these other fees. The reduced rate fees are roughly 75 percent of the full fees. The half-time rates are roughly 60 percent (three-fifths) of the full-time rates. The three-day rates fall anywhere from 73 percent to 75 percent of the full-time rates. It is helpful to use market data for less than full-time schedules if you can obtain comparable numbers. This information helps to keep your rates more competitive.

Now you have a starting point for your tuition fee structure. In Chapter 4, we will see how to work with these rates so that they bring in enough revenue to cover the costs of doing business.

PUTTING IT ALL TOGETHER AND KEEPING IT THERE

Once you have a fee structure and have defined the school's enrollment capacity, you will want to review these configurations on an annual basis probably around the time you are building your budget. You will want to evaluate your fee structure to determine whether

- your rates are still close to the competition
- the relationship between full-time and part-time rates still makes sense
- your rates are too low and are not *at least* covering the full current cost of care
- your rates are too high and are discouraging enrollment.

✓ Hint

It is important to review your fee structure and enrollment offerings annually.

You will also constantly be monitoring your enrollment and working to anticipate changes in demand for your services, being open to considering modifications to the schedules you offer or the age groups you serve in order to better serve your community. Recruiting and retention of qualified staff will be the next large issue you face.

REFERENCES

National Resource Center for Health and Safety in Child Care database, accessed June 30, 2003, http://www.nrc.uchsc.edu

Willer, B. (Ed.). (1990). *Reaching the full cost of quality in early childhood programs*. Washington, DC: NAEYC. Use of the material from *Reaching the Full Cost of Quality* by permission of NAEYC.

Willer, B. (1990). Estimating the full cost of quality. In B. Willer (Ed.). *Reaching the full cost of quality in early childhood programs* (pp. 55–86). Washington, DC: NAEYC.

HELPFUL WEB SITES

http://www.naeyc.org

Web site of the National Association of the Education of Young Children, with links to state organizations.

http://www.nrc.uchsc.edu

Web site of the National Resource Center for Health and Safety, which lists all child care licensing regulations by state.

Staffing: A Guide to Recruitment and Retention

MAKING YOUR PROGRAM A GOOD PLACE TO WORK

In the first chapter, we talked a bit about the working environment, or climate, in your center, and how you as the manager have the power to influence that climate. Is your program a good place to work? What makes it a place where child development professionals want to spend their day?

One of the specific areas you can affect that will help create a positive climate and make your program a place that attracts early childhood educators is staff compensation. The compensation I am talking about here includes wages, benefits, professional development, recognition, and respect.

DETERMINING WHAT YOU NEED, WHAT YOU WANT, AND WHAT YOU CAN AFFORD

If you have gone through the process of determining the minimum requirements you need for your teaching staff and have looked at what changes you might make to provide even better staffing coverage (as discussed in Chapter 2), you will want to calculate what the cost of these levels of staffing will be. That process begins with the determination of wages for staff. The process for determining staff wages is similar to the one we use to set tuition rates. As you compile your budget (see Chapter 4), you will be able to determine if the level of staffing you currently have is too great—i.e., if you have too many teachers for the enrollment at your program, or their rate of pay is too high—or if you have an inadequate number of staff.

Staff Wages

In order to design a structure for staff wages, or to evaluate the one you are already using, you will want to consult a market survey that gives you the most up-to-date information on what child care salaries are in your community. The Center for the Child Care Workforce (CCW), headquartered in Washington, D.C., has surveyed salary and benefit information for every state. For some states, CCW has also gathered information by county. This data is available from them in printed form or on the Internet. The last survey was completed by CCW in 2000 and is available on their Web site at <http://www.ccw.org> (see Appendix C). I have found that the data provided by CCW is usually the most current, the most accurate, and the easiest to access of any other child care salary data I have seen.

You could also conduct your own local survey to determine what other child care agencies are paying their staff. Three or four other comparable organizations are probably enough. However, if you are uncomfortable calling for this information, or if you find that others are reluctant to share this information with you, you should rely on the comparable data that has already been published. Data that is older than the current year's is much better than no data at all. Sometimes, advertisements for teachers in the newspaper will list the rate of pay.

Wages should be based on the education and experience of each teacher. Experience can mean not only how long a teacher has worked in *your* program, but also how many years of *comparable* experience she had prior to becoming your employee. I want to credit teachers with some number of years' experience if that experience has been at another quality center, working with a similar age group. By following your state's credentialing requirements, you can develop a wage grid to display a wage range for each educational level obtained by the teacher, and the wage increases for that level of education for each year of experience.

Figures 3–1 and 3–2 are examples of wage grids for teaching staff at two different child care facilities. As teachers complete higher levels of education and/or additional years of experience, they move to a higher wage rate. This wage information can be openly discussed with your staff, so that everyone understands what is required to earn a particular wage. All employees know that you are working from one set of numbers applied equitably to everyone, and that when a new teacher is hired her wage rate is based on the same grid.

In Figure 3–1, all teaching staff are hired at the starting rate without regard to previous experience. They can advance on the matrix by completing more education and for each year they work at the center. In the second figure (3–2), the hiring wage for the teacher depends on their past experience as well as their education. For more years of equivalent teaching experience, a new teacher may be hired at a step higher than the "starting" wage rate. They can enter the grid at any point upon hiring.

Unless you are the owner of your own program, someone else will determine your salary. For others on the administrative staff, you will need to develop a separate wage schedule. It should be based on wage rates that are competitive in your community and comparable to other "office" jobs, even though you may be hiring someone for the office who is an early childhood educator. The best information is usually available through local community databases (ask at your library), or by scanning ads in the newspaper. This data will tell you what wages are being paid locally. The U.S. Department of Labor's *Occupational Outlook Handbook* is another source of comparable wage data and is available online (see Appendix C). This database is a report of the *median* salaries (meaning half of the salaries surveyed are below this number and half are above this number) of every profession you can imagine in the United States. The only problem with this information, and it may be a significant problem for you, is that national averages are not really representative if you live in an area with a high cost of living or an extremely low cost of living. For example, the national

Wage Matrix 1
Hourly Wage Rates

Position	Starting Hourly Wage	Step 1	Step 2	Step 3
Teaching Assistant NO UNITS to Minimally Qualified	$8.50	$8.63–$8.76	$8.76–$9.02	**
Teacher* Core 12 ECE Units	$9.50	$9.64–$9.79	$9.79–$10.08	**
15–24 ECE Units (Core + Admin)	$10.50	$10.66–$10.82	$10.82–$11.14	**
CD Permit and/or AA in ECE	$11.50	$11.67–$11.85	$11.85–$12.21	**
Head Teacher* CD Permit + Supervision of Adults	$12.00	$12.18–$12.36	$12.36–$12.73	**
BA with CD Permit or Site Supervisor Permit	$12.50	$12.69–$12.88	$12.88–$13.27	**
Substitutes 0–12 ECE Units	$10.00			
Teacher Qualified	$11.00			

* Must have infant/toddler development course to work in toddler room.

** There is a step increase for each year worked at the center.
Each step is 1.5% COLA and up to an additional 1.5% based
on performance and merit. Merit is defined as employees'
participation in activities, meetings, and fundraising events.

All raises are contingent on funding availability.

FIGURE 3–1 Sample Wage Matrix

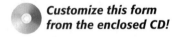

***Customize this form
from the enclosed CD!***

average annual salary for a preschool teacher in the year 2000 was listed in the *Occupational Outlook Handbook* as $17,810. The 2002 report by the Center for the Child Care Workforce, with data collected in 2000 also, reports that in Santa Cruz, California, the average annual child care teacher salary ranged from $18,845 to $23,670. The national average from the *Occupational Outlook Handbook* does not really help me if I am setting salaries for teachers in Santa Cruz. Keeping that in mind, however, you may still be able to use this information as another data point in determining a reasonable wage for your staff.

Once you have constucted a salary grid for your teaching staff, you may want to run a reality check of the wages of your current staff against this grid. You may find that either the grid is way out of line with what you are paying, or that some of the wages earned by staff do not fit in the matrix where they should, based on an employee's educational level or years of experience. Adjustments to the grid, or to the individual's wage rate (adjusting upward only), should be made until you are comfortable that your wage matrix accurately reflects what your teachers are earning.

	Years of Experience	(Teaching Assistant) 0–11 ECE Credits	BA Degree or 12–23 ECE Units	Education 24 ECE Units	CD Permit or AA in ECE	BA in ECE	MA in ECE
			Wage Matrix 2 Hourly Wage Rates				
0–1		$8.00	$9.00–$10.00	$9.50–$11.00	$10.00–$12.00	$11.00–$13.00	$12.00–$14.00
1–3		$8.24	$9.27–$10.30	$9.79–$11.33	$10.30–$12.36	$11.33–$13.39	$12.36–$14.42
3–5		$8.49	$9.55–$10.61	$10.08–$11.67	$10.61–$12.73	$11.67–$13.79	$12.73–$14.85
5–7		$8.74	$9.83–$10.93	$10.39–$12.02	$10.93–$13.11	$12.02–$14.20	$13.11–$15.30
7–9		$9.00	$10.12–$11.26	$10.70–$12.38	$11.26–$13.51	$12.38–$14.63	$13.51–$15.76
9–12		$9.27	$10.42–$11.60	$11.02–$12.75	$11.60–$13.92	$12.75–$15.07	$13.92–$16.23
12–15		$9.55	$10.74–$11.95	$11.35–$13.13	$11.95–$14.33	$13.13–$15.52	$14.33–$16.72
15+		$9.84	$11.06–$12.31	$11.69–$13.52	$12.31–$14.76	$13.52–$15.99	$14.76–$17.22

FIGURE 3–2 Sample Wage Matrix 2

It is never advisable to hire new staff at a higher rate than staff already working in your program with similar backgrounds in education and experience. Although you may be tempted in a tight job market to offer a candidate a higher wage to secure the "perfect" teacher, it is inevitable that your teachers will find out. When they do, you will have a difficult time trying to reestablish their trust that you are committed to fair and equitable treatment among staff.

Benefits

As important to recruiting and retaining qualified staff as *salaries*, staff *benefits* are a part of the total compensation picture. Benefits can even be considered "payment" to your employees, but they are a kind of payment that is not taxed. Because the salaries in our industry are relatively low compared to similar job classifications in other industries, the provision of a good benefit package can help attract teachers to your program and keep them there. Some of the benefits you may want to consider for your compensation package include:

- health insurance
- dental insurance
- vision insurance
- retirement plan
- paid holidays
- paid vacation time
- paid sick time
- child care discount
- paid planning time
- paid prep time
- paid bereavement leave

✓ Hint

Offering paid benefits to staff can be just as important for recruiting and retaining qualified employees as providing an adequate wage rate.

There is, of course, a cost associated with each of these benefits. Whereas offering a three-day paid bereavement leave to all staff when there is a death in the family would cost the center very little, providing health insurance to all employees can be very costly, running in the tens of thousands of dollars annually. Some kind of benefit package is essential if you are hoping to attract the best candidates to your program. As a bare *minimum*, I recommend including:

- paid holidays
- paid vacation/sick days
- health insurance with a copay

To me, the rationale for paying for holidays is obvious. If your families are paying monthly or weekly tuition, they are usually paying for all national holidays during which you are closed. Your enrollment revenue is already paying staff for these days. The justification for paid vacation and sick days is less obvious, although just as important. Teachers, especially, will get sick, and will need time away from their job. At child care wages, few teachers can afford to take time off unless they are paid for this time. This is time well earned, for which staff should be compensated. It is time that is already computed in their annual salary, but the additional cost of hiring substitutes when teachers are sick or on vacation must be considered. Two to three weeks' vacation per year should be standard practice in programs that operate during 12 months of the year.

Rather than offering separate bundles of vacation days and sick days, you may want to consider having paid days in one bundle of **personal time off (PTO)** days. If employees earn, for example, 10 vacation days a year and 5 sick days, their PTO benefit would be 15 days per year. If an employee is not sick all year, she can use the total 15 days as vacation. On the flip side, if an employee is out due to illness a lot, he will have very few paid vacation days to use. Under employment law, all vacation time an employee accrues, or earns, must be paid to that employee when he leaves his employment. Sick days, by contrast, are lost if they are not used by the employee and do not have to be paid to employees when they leave.

Even though not all child care programs offer their employees health insurance, it is a benefit that will distinguish your program from others and it will help attract the kind of employees you want for your center. If you are concerned about controlling the cost of health insurance (or any other kind of insurance), you may want to consider offering each eligible employee a fixed percentage of the cost of their coverage. For example, if the monthly cost of providing health insurance varies by age of employee and looks something like this,

Ages up to 30	$120/month
Ages 31–39	$150/month
Ages 40–49	$175/month
Ages 50–59	$210/month
Ages 60+	$270/month,

the health insurance benefit you offer can be a flat percentage of each employee's premium. The part the employee will pay is then the difference between what your center pays and the cost of the insurance. In all small businesses the trend is toward sharing the cost of health insurance with employees, rather than reducing the quality of insurance or eliminating it altogether. As costs of these programs increase every year, the increase can be shared between employees and employers.

! TIP

Comparison shopping for the best, most affordable medical insurance for your employees will not cost anything and it may save you money.

It is worth your time to shop for health insurance, either with the assistance of an insurance broker that specializes in small businesses or through direct contact with health insurance providers. You can obtain a free quote for cost of insurance usually by sending in a census of your employees. A census is a list of all employees and their vital statistics. Many large providers, such as Blue Cross/Blue Shield, have their own Web sites where you can obtain a quote on line for your program.

Your state may offer health insurance coverage for small businesses, in which you are included in a pool of other organizations. Employees often gain more choices with this kind of coverage, and you receive only one bill each month for all employees and all plans they have selected.

In order to determine what benefits you should be offering to your employees, it may be helpful to ask everyone working in your program what benefits they want. A simple survey can ask employees to rank the benefits from a list you have created of only those benefits *you would be willing*, or which *you are permitted*, to consider providing. If there is a list of six kinds of benefits—for example,

- health insurance with copay
- dental insurance with copay
- paid holidays
- paid vacation and sick days
- paid vision plan
- child care discount

—employees rank the benefits on this list from one to six, where "one" indicates their first choice. By tallying all the responses, you will have a ranking of the benefits that the employees choose. You can work down the list beginning with their first choice to secure the benefits your program can afford. Then, perhaps annually, you ask the same question again as you are preparing your budget. You will see whether current employees have the same needs and you can determine what benefits you may want to add or alter.

Obviously, in some situations, the benefits offered to employees are determined by corporate or governmental policy and employees are not asked about their preferences. However, if you feel the benefit package for employees could be improved, you may still want to conduct your own survey and forward this information to your managers with a recommendation for adding or changing the benefits offered.

FINDING QUALIFIED STAFF

Depending on where you live and work and what is happening in your local economy, it may be easy or difficult to recruit qualified staff for your facility. When there are a lot of people looking for jobs, candidates will find you as long as your program has a visible presence in the community. If unemployment is low and your competition is hiring, then you must be more creative in how you find teacher candidates.

Advertising

You probably know about advertising. Most programs have used advertising in one form or another to attract candidates. It is usually expensive, unless you are able to find free or low-cost avenues for advertising your open positions. In our community, a free daily newspaper offered classified advertising rates well below the cost for larger papers. Because it was a free paper and distributed widely through the local community, it had a large readership of people either living locally or who came into the community to work. We were very successful using this paper as our only paid advertising. Other papers were too expensive and not very effective for the short time span we could afford to run an ad. It was through a process of trial and error that we learned which newspaper ads brought us the highest number of qualified responses.

Free advertising sources are also usually available. Check out local employment services, which often post job openings for no fee. Our center was able to post job openings at no cost with a local service called the Career Action Center. We also sent job flyers to all the local community college child development departments for posting and to the state employment development department's on-line postings. When there is time to develop relationships with colleges in your neighborhood, county, and state—through mentor teacher programs or providing student teacher placement—it can help you attract these future candidates to your center.

Posting job openings online has become a standard practice. You may find this works well for you, or works well for a period of time, but it can be expensive. During a period when we had several openings for all levels of teaching staff and also needed an administrator, we used HotJobs®, an Internet listing of job openings and resumes. A contract with HotJobs for three months cost us $525 per month. This contract allowed us to advertise up to five jobs, search their database of resumes, and edit our job listings as frequently as we wanted. The downside to this kind of advertising is of course the high cost, but also the wide exposure. We received responses from candidates all over the world (literally!), when what we really wanted was to find someone locally who was qualified for the positions. I did hire two exceptional women who responded to our HotJobs ads. One lived in Tennesse at the time, and one lived in Utah. They were both completing their master's degrees in child development, and wanted to relocate to California. They were hired in 1998, and both worked at our center for over five years. It is at least worth exploring Internet-based advertising if you can afford it. It may work for you.

Job Fairs

Though I have never really been successful recruiting new staff through job fairs at colleges and universities, I would still recommend them. First of all, it is usually free or requires only a small fee to participate in a job fair. Secondly, over time, appearing at job fairs in your community helps to get your program better known. It is also an excellent opportunity to train yourself and members of your staff to talk about your organization and introduce potential candidates to what you do and why they should work for you. And, finally, maybe most important of all, I always enjoyed the opportunity to network with other programs, big and small, who were my competitors in the community, and see what they were offering to teacher candidates.

Open Houses

Another advertising option is an open house for teacher candidates. Like job fairs, open houses can increase your presence in the community, and *over time* bring you the kind of reputation that will eventually draw good teacher candidates to your site. It can be done during a school day when candidates can see what your program looks and feels like in operation. Or it can also be done on a weekend when potential candidates may have more time to come, and when you can collect resumes and talk with individuals without distraction.

Word of Mouth

The least expensive and most effective means of finding new employees is through word of mouth. Make sure everyone you talk to knows that you are looking for a teacher, or an office

! TIP

Never underestimate the value of word-of-mouth publicity in finding the right candidate for your staff.

assistant, or whatever the open position may be. Let your staff know too, and encourage them to spread the word in child development workshops or classes they may be attending. They may even have a friend who is working in another program but is not happy with her job and is looking for a change. During the late 1990s, when recruiting for new teachers in the San Francisco Bay area was the most difficult, our program offered a $500 bonus to any staff member who referred a teacher candidate to us who was eventually hired and stayed for at least six months. I considered this an advertising cost and well worth the expense if it helped me find a good teacher. I was happier paying a staff member for her referral than paying a fee to a newspaper.

HIRING

What happens after you have placed an employment advertisement or conducted an open house for new teachers? Hopefully you will receive a number of resumes from qualified candidates. You will want to evaluate the resumes and screen the candidates for the qualifications for which you are hiring. When you have selected the applicants you wish to interview, not more than five and hopefully more than one, the hiring process begins.

Interviews

In my preparation for writing this book, I discovered a lot of business advice about interviewing job applicants. Also, I did a lot of interviewing myself as director of a large child care facility. If you are new to this task you may want to do some research and reading on the subject just to get you started. The "how-to" of conducting an interview can be learned by following expert advice or example and then refining the technique you will use that works best in your organization.

✓ Hint

Involve other staff in interviews of candidates and hiring decisions to help assure the selection of the right employee.

What I do not think can be taught, however, is the "gut-feeling" of knowing when you have the right candidate for your job. I have known colleagues who are very good at knowing who to hire. I have made some excellent choices in hiring, but I have also made some poor decisions and hired candidates who were never suited for our program. Accept the fact you may not always make the right decision. By involving others on your staff in the hiring process, however, you may be able to increase your chances of finding the right person to hire. Instead of only having one voice (your own) to make the hiring decision, you will have two or three other opinions about the applicants. Each person involved in the hiring process will notice aspects of the applicants that others did not.

In my child care organization, two or three of us were usually involved in the initial interviews and development of interview questions. Some of the questions we used appear in Figure 3–3. We alternated asking the questions, although at any time during the interview, any one of us could ask a question not on the list. We encouraged the candidates to ask us any questions they had. Each one of us took separate notes.

There are certain questions that are illegal to ask candidates in an interview or to ask on a job application. Federal and state labor laws are designed to protect individuals from discrimination based on their personal characteristics. Following is a list of the type of questions you may not ask.

- What is your date of birth? / How old are you?
- What is your marital status?
- What is your religion?
- Do you have children?

Interview Questions

1. Tell us a little bit about your educational background.

2. Tell us a little bit about your experience in early childhood education.

3. Describe a work situation where you had to work with a teacher that had a different philosophy about how children learn and tell us how you handled it.

4. Describe your philosophy about how children learn.

5. What kind of positive guidance techniques have you found to work with young children?

6. How would you respond in the following situation:

   a. You are working with a group of three-year-olds. One child has just had a toilet accident and comes over to you and is crying.

   b. One of your four-year-olds, who has recently joined the class, is very reluctant to join other children in any play activities.

   c. A parent approaches you at the end of the day to ask why her child's clothes are covered in paint.

7. What age group do you most enjoy working with and why?

FIGURE 3–3 Interview Questions

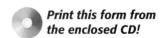

Print this form from the enclosed CD!

Immediately following the interview one of us gave the candidate a tour of our center and introduced her to staff members as we went from room to room. Not only was this an opportunity for the candidates to see our facility and meet some of the other staff, but it gave us the opportunity to observe the interactions between each candidate and other teachers and children we might meet during the tour.

When time permitted, the interview committee would assemble immediately following each interview and tour. We discussed each applicant while their presence and responses to our interview questions were still fresh in our memory. We were often able at this point to determine whether we could eliminate a candidate from further consideration or whether we felt she should be one of the final candidates. One of us would take on the task of calling the candidates' references and verifying schools attended and degrees awarded.

Making the Hiring Decision

Once we had interviewed all the initial candidates and selected the final group of not more than three applicants, the classroom team for which we were hiring was brought into the hiring process. The candidates spent time in the classroom and with the lead teacher. The final selection was made after all of the finalists had a chance to visit in the room and we had all discussed the pros and cons of each candidate.

The choice of the final selection will not always be unanimous. My advice, when there is a disagreement about who to hire, is to allow the teaching team to make the choice. If the initial interview screening results in two or three finalists who are all qualified for the position, then you, as administrator, should be content with the selection of any of the three. It is then important to make a choice of the one candidate that the team prefers. Feelings of connection and compatibility to one of the candidates are important to consider since the goal is to develop a group of teachers that work together as a team.

On some occasions, you may have to make the final choice. You should be very clear with the teachers that you want and welcome their feedback on the candidates, but that you will be making the final decision. If, for example, you are seeking particular strengths in a new teacher that may be lacking in other teachers on the team, your choice of candidate may not be the one who *feels* the most compatible to the team.

Offer Letter

When you have made a decision to hire someone, the offer of a position can be made over the telephone. At this time, you can tell the candidate you will put all the relevant information in a letter to him. He may want to wait until receipt of the letter to tell you whether he is accepting the offer, or he may tell you on the phone. The letter, however, should always be sent out so that both you and the new teacher have the terms of her employment in writing. A sample offer letter appears in Figure 3–4. The letter should contain the specifics of the appointment, including:

- job title and room assignment
- rate of pay
- work hours
- benefits for which she is eligible and when they begin

Sample Offer Letter

Felton Family Preschool
6500 Highway 9
Felton, CA 95018

July 12, 2003

Dear New Teacher:

As we discussed on the telephone this morning, I would like to offer you the position of teacher in the Toddler Room at the Felton Family Preschool beginning on Monday, July 22, 2003. You will be working thirty (30) hours per week from 11:30 in the morning until 6:00 p.m., Monday through Friday, with a 30-minute unpaid lunch break. Your starting salary will be $11.25 per hour.

As part of your compensation package, you are also eligible for the following benefits, which become effective 60 days after your hire date:

- health insurance
- dental insurance
- 10 paid holidays per year
- 5 paid sick days per year
- 10 paid vacation days per year

We are delighted to offer you this position, and hope you will accept our offer. Please let me know no later than July 17 whether you will accept. Thank you very much.

Sincerely,

Ms. Director

FIGURE 3–4 Sample Offer Letter

If he has not yet accepted the position, you should also include a date by which you require a response to the offer.

PERSONNEL POLICIES AND PROCEDURES

If your program employs more than a few staff members, it is necessary to have written personnel policies and procedures in an employee handbook.

Employee Handbooks

You can write the employee handbook yourself, or if your center already has one, you can review it annually and make any necessary changes or updates. You want to keep this document up to date to reflect changes in any of your policies or changes in labor laws. It is *the* document you may have to refer to if there are any personnel disputes in your organization. It is the document that all employees should have in their possession for answers to questions on personnel issues.

At a minimum, an employee handbook should include the following sections, not necessarily in this order:

> welcome to new staff
>
> statement of center philosophy
>
> Equal Opportunity Employer (EOE) declaration
>
> nondiscrimination policy
>
> nonharassment policy
>
> staff compensation
>
> job descriptions
>
> health and maternity leave policies
>
> employee conduct policy
>
> employee grievance policy
>
> employee discipline policy

Every new employee should receive a copy of the employee handbook when they are hired. If the handbook is prepared as pages in a loose-leaf notebook, it is easy to modify parts of the handbook and only replace the pages that are affected when you are making changes. *All* pages should have the date they were prepared listed at the bottom. When major revisions are made, the entire handbook can be reprinted.

There are many sources to consult if you are preparing your own handbook. Books and software programs that include templates for all of these topics can be purchased (see Appendix C). Your state department of labor can also provide you with their requirements for labor policies, usually as a poster, which should be displayed for all employees to view.

Job Descriptions

A job description for each of the job categories in your program should be included in the employee handbook. These job descriptions serve to clarify what is expected of each employee in their role as, for example, head teacher, teacher, or teaching assistant. To be most helpful to you as the supervisor, and to the employees, these descriptions should list the specific duties of the job in some detail. The more essential details you are able to provide, the less confusion there will be in knowing what an employee is responsible for and what is expected of her. When questions arise as to whether someone is "doing their job," or as to how well they are doing their job, you have a written document to which you can refer and which is the same for all employees in that job category. If possible, however, try to keep your descriptions to one page each. When descriptions are too long, they are harder to write and harder to read. Excessive detail precludes the flexibility we want lead teachers to have to distribute tasks within their group to best meet the needs of their classroom. You also want a teacher job description to describe equally well the work of a teacher with each age group in your center.

An example of a job description for a teacher at the Felton Family Preschool appears in Figure 3–5. Notice that in addition to a fairly well-detailed description of duties, there is also a summary of the qualifications required for this job. A second sample job description appearing in Figure 3–6 comes from *Policies and Procedures for Early Childhood Directors* (pp. 127–128), written by the Early Childhood Directors Association. Another excellent source of detailed job descriptions for early childhood is *Blueprint for Action* (Bloom, Sheerer, and Britz, 1991). In this informative and extensive work about staff development there is a detailed job description for a preschool teacher, and short, summary descriptions for master teacher, teacher, assistant teacher, teacher aide, early childhood special educator, parent education coordinator, social service coordinator, education coordinator, and program administrator. Any of these descriptions can be adapted to the particular needs of your own program.

Performance Reviews

Performance reviews with staff can be mutually enjoyable and beneficial experiences. The key to encouraging a positive encounter is in the way you think about performance appraisals. If you and your staff think of them as opportunities to criticize an employee's work and to insist on corrections, then your performance reviews will fail and no one will want to participate. If, on the other hand, performance reviews are seen as a chance to reflect on and discuss a teacher's work over the past time period (six months, one year), then both you and your employees will anticipate this event eagerly. Reviews should be used to inform all participants of the teachers' strengths as well as their weaknesses. They are also opportunities for staff to evaluate their own performance. Employees should look at aspects of their performance where they feel they need improvement and set goals for themselves for the coming year. Then the employee and administrator are able to plan together how to accomplish these goals.

The most comprehensive explanation of this kind of approach to performance reviews appears in *Blueprint for Action* (pp. 121–135). Sample forms for

- preparing for a review
- creating a list of goals
- creating an action plan to accomplish these goals

are included in Appendix A and on the CD enclosed with the *Business of Child Care*. A detailed example of this process is included in Chapter 7.

So through this process you are really doing two things: you are permitting and encouraging each employee to reflect on her own work and then articulate her needs based on this reflection, while at the same time you are evaluating her past performance against the criteria of the job specifications you want her to achieve. When it is time to formulate a set of goals to work on, these two sides of looking at performance come together. Reviews of

---

Felton Family Preschool

Teacher Job Description

Summary

The teacher is part of a classroom teaching team that is responsible for the care and education of the students. She is supervised by the Head Teacher on the team. The teacher is responsible for preparing and implementing developmentally-appropriate curriculum activities for the class, for assessment of the needs of the children, and for communication with parents.

Specific Responsibilities

- Provides a safe, clean environment in the classroom.
- Organizes and cleans materials available to children.
- Plans a healthy snack menu.
- Promotes the physical development of all of the children by providing frequent opportunity for large motor play both inside and outside.
- Provides a good balance of quiet and active learning activities.
- Supports child-initiated play.
- Promotes the social and emotional development of all the children through positive guidance.
- Regularly conducts assessments of children and uses this information to plan classroom activities.
- Establishes a partnership with parents to support the needs of each child.
- Encourages parents to participate in the classroom.
- Conducts annual parent conferences.
- Mentors teaching assistants and helps orient and guide new staff and substitutes working in the classroom.
- Attends all staff meetings.
- Participates in professional development activities.
- Works cooperatively and communicates openly with all members of his teaching team.
- Works cooperatively and communicates openly with all employees at the center.

Qualifications

BA degree in child development or related field. OR, AA degree in child development plus 2 years' teaching experience in a center-based child care program. OR, 24 ECE semester units and 3 years' teaching experience in a center-based child care program.

FIGURE 3–5 Felton Family Preschool Teacher Job Description

employees should always occur in an atmosphere of give and take, where you are doing as much or more *listening to* as you are *talking to* your teachers.

Regular performance appraisals are a good thing for your program. Mark your calendar for anniversary dates of each employee's hire date and schedule these reviews at least once a year, more often for new staff members. Be sure to make notes all year long concerning observations you've made of an employee performing well and of things you observed that were of concern to you. File the notes in the employee's personnel file, so prior to the annual

Teacher Job Description

Qualifications

The person selected for this position must possess the educational qualifications of a teacher as outlined by state requirements. This person must have a warm, friendly personality, be sensitive to the feelings and needs of others, be able to relate well with children, and be willing to fulfill job responsibilities in accordance with the program philosophy. The person must be able to maintain a professional attitude toward the children, the families, and the staff at all times, and be able to communicate professionally and openly.

The person should be a model, demonstrating the kinds of values, attitudes, expectations, beliefs, and choices that make our organization excellent.

Responsibilities include but are not limited to the following:

1. Assist the program director in long-range planning with regard to curriculum, the program's philosophy, and goals.

2. Complete monthly, weekly, and daily curriculum plans in time for the group and communicate these plans to assistant teachers and aides, and if needed, to program's other teachers.

3. Plan, prepare, and implement a curriculum that is appropriate for the age level, skill, and social development of the group of children served.

4. Supervise and interact with the children in all areas of the program, outdoors, and during field trips away from the program.

5. Maintain an environment that helps each child to have a positive experience throughout the school day.

6. Treat all children with dignity and respect and allow for individual differences.

7. Be familiar with and adhere to the program's policies, health and safety regulations, and emergency procedures, and be ready to implement these if necessary.

8. Assist the program director to orient, train, and supervise aides, assistant teachers, and substitutes.

9. Help assistant teachers and aides to maintain a professional attitude toward the program, the children, and the staff, and assist if needed with appropriate communication. Be an example of professional behavior and appropriate communication at all times.

10. Plan, prepare, and care for the environment.

11. Be responsible for maintaining the observational records for each child and all other routine forms.

12. Be responsible for accomplishing all routine tasks with regard to the health and safety of the children and the maintenance of the program in accordance with local and state regulations.

13. Attend all staff meetings and recommend training programs and conferences. Provide the director with documentation in accordance with state requirements. Provide appropriate communication in staff meetings and assist in designing appropriate training opportunities for staff.

14. Be an advocate for improvement of early childhood education and for improving our program.

15. Maintain an open, friendly, professional relationship with all families. Set up conferences as needed.

FIGURE 3–6 Teacher Job Description

Schedule regular performance reviews with all employees on the anniversary of their hire date.

appraisal you have these notes to read to help you remember what you know about this employee.

Most employees I supervised really wanted the opportunity to meet with me to talk about themselves and their job. Just the fact that I had made time for the review indicated to the employee I was interested in them and wanted to know how they were doing and what they were thinking. Because there was a list of questions to answer before their meeting with me, they had some idea of what to expect at the meeting. They could prepare themselves for what they wanted to say and could prepare any documentation they might have that highlighted their work over the year. We often talked about their plans for the future: whether they wanted to work with a different age group, whether they wanted to work with a different teaching team, what kind of professional development opportunities they needed. My undivided and individual attention told my staff that they were an important part of the school's community.

Discipline

Did you arrive at this section directly after searching the table of contents or index? Is this your "hot button"? I know that it is a topic that concerns a lot of child care administrators. We fear having to discipline our staff and so we avoid doing it. We try not to see when an employee is consistently late to arrive, or we ignore it when we observe an infant teacher change a diaper without once speaking to the child. (I've avoided both issues at one time.)

But, as you all know, discipline is something that every administrator in every child care program will have to face. Ignoring behavior that is incompatible with the goals of your program can have very damaging effects. Poorly performing individuals provide poor care to children. Teachers who do not communicate openly with their team create anger and division among the staff. When they fail to discipline in these instances, resentment builds among those individuals who work hard and do their jobs well. They wonder, if a co-teacher is always late arriving or coming back from his breaks and is never reprimanded for it, why should I try so hard to be on time? When a teacher speaks about one of the parents in front of other teachers and management seems not to care, why am I trying so hard to maintain positive relationships with parents who are very difficult? My supervisor never appreciates or recognizes my effort.

The business section of your library or bookstore is the best place to look for books that can help you learn how to discipline employees who are not performing well. A few that I would recommend are discussed below.

Dealing with Problem Employees: *A Legal Guide,* by Amy Delps and Lisa Guerin.
A well-written and easy-to-read book. Not only does it give you sound advice about how to talk to people whose behavior you are trying to change, it also includes some basic information on employment law. Some key topics include:

- defining the problem
- basic employment law, and state-by-state differences
- performance evaluations
- discipline
- firing—how to fire; what to say

The A-to-Z Guide of Managing People, by Victoria Kaplan and Robert Kunreuther.
What I like about this particular book is the explanation by the authors of the distinction between *discipline problems* that involve your program's rules and policies, versus *job performance problems* that involve an employee's knowledge, skills, and abilities. If

an employee is not perfoming her job adequately, you cannot discipline this employee into doing a better job. An employee may be lacking some specific training, which when received will allow that employee to do a better job.

Why Employees Don't Do What They're Supposed To Do, by Ferdinand F. Foumies.
This is also a very easy-to-read book. You can pick it up and read any chapter on its own. Each chapter discusses one of the sixteen reasons why employees don't perform, based on Mr. Foumies's research. He gives you his "preventive management" strategies to use to solve each of these performance problems.

Because so many other authors have written so well about working with nonperforming employees, I will not do so here. But I want to reiterate the importance of talking with your employees throughout the year about their performance, both good and bad, and making notes for their personnel file, so when it does come time for their review there will be no surprises concerning what you will be talking about. If an employee does exhibit more serious problems that should be disciplined, don't wait for review time, but face the employee promptly and directly. If an employee has performance issues, again don't wait for her review to talk about it. Try to find ways to provide more training for her, or consider reconfiguring her job to better suit her abilities.

OTHER GOOD THINGS FOR STAFF

Once you have been able to establish a basically friendly and comfortable environment for your staff and have developed a staff compensation package, and you have recruited and hired enough teachers and office personnel, you may have a little time to consider some of the following additional features that will enhance the organizational climate.

New Staff Orientation

Over the years of being an administrator I have learned that the establishment of a planned program to orient new staff members is well worth the effort. Instead of tossing a new teacher into the classroom on her first day and expecting her to know her role, I would encourage you to consider a different approach. Pay the new employee for her first day of work, but instead of her working in her own classroom, provide her with an orientation program where she

- spends some time reading her employee handbook and then reviews with you what is in it,
- spends some time with you (or other office staff) learning where things are at the center, how to submit his hours for payroll, how to request time off, etc.,
- spends some time in each of the other classrooms, helping out and getting to know the other teachers.

This process may take less than one whole day depending on the size of your program, or may take a day and a half. The time is a good investment for you in that it provides all new employees with accurate information about their role as a teacher and the workings of your program from the very beginning of their employment. It allows you to begin to develop a relationship with each new staff member. It helps them get to know other members of your staff and for your staff to get to know the new employee before he is forever confined to his own classroom. I have also been successful in assigning a staff "buddy" to a new employee. The buddy's job is to be available to answer any questions the new teacher may have, to sit with her at lunch, and to generally make her feel that she is welcome as part of the community.

Professional Development

The inclusion of a professional development program in your center is another important piece of creating an organizational climate that values its employees. It serves your needs of wanting the most qualified employees to care for the children in your program. It serves the needs of the employees who will gain personal satisfaction and fulfillment and greater skills through more training. It should be considered a requirement of working in your program that all employees are always engaged in some form of professional development.

A program of ongoing professional development does not have to cost a lot of money. It can include any of the following kinds of training:

- on-site staff seminars and workshops
- visits to other programs
- attendance at professional conferences, workshops, etc.
- classes at the local community college
- communication skills workshop
- first aid/CPR classes

Many school-supply vendors will provide training in their products to your staff at no or low cost.

Your staff development program can be designed as an outcome of the performance appraisals and goal setting you have done with your staff. It should be directly connected to the needs of your staff as you determine at a point in time. If no one on staff particularly needs the "Music and Movement" class, don't waste money on it. Instead, you may want to bring in a first-aid trainer once a year and require all staff to attend. If you have employees who have particular skills that can be shared with other employees, ask them to conduct a "brown bag" workshop over the lunchtime for any employees who want to attend. One of my head teachers is a particularly creative art instructor. She provided a lunchtime hands-on workshop for teachers where she shared her techniques for using found and free material to create two- and three-dimensional art. Ask staff what kinds of training they want and ask staff what kinds of training they can provide.

Staff Recognition

Find ways to compliment your staff. This shouldn't be difficult. It makes everyone feel good and feel valued. By being specific in your comments, employees know exactly what behavior is being praised. Do it on the spot, e.g., as you are walking through the toddler room and observe a teacher speaking gently to a toddler who is crying. "I really like the way you are speaking to Sam. I can see he has a very caring teacher." Try to do it for everyone. Try to find something positive you notice and comment on for everyone on your staff at least once a week. This can become a habit that soon will be second nature to you.

Learn to compliment yourself too, because you may not hear a lot of positive recognition from your employees or parents. "I really did a good job talking with John's parents. It was a difficult subject to bring up, but I think I helped them understand what we are trying to do and how we want their help."

Preparation Time and Meeting Time

Less easy to provide and much more costly than frequent, verbal recognition, is paid time for staff to prepare the classroom in the morning before children arrive, to clean up at

! TIP

Regular, positive feedback to members of your staff is an invaluable investment in the welfare of the human resources that make your program what it is.

the end of the day after children leave, and to attend team meetings. For many programs, these are luxuries that do not fit in the budget. If it is possible to provide any of these, however, they should be considered as staff benefits because they add to the positive climate in a child care organization. This kind of paid time away from children helps all teachers provide better care to children, and also helps to keep teachers sane. Sometimes it is possible to find periods during naptime when a teacher can use an extra half hour to prepare an activity, or call parents, or meet with another teacher, away from children. At one center where I worked, we had a monthly staff meeting that all staff were required to attend. It was held in the evening so I did have to pay overtime wages to some of our staff. We usually allowed only one half hour for centerwide business. The remaining hour was left for classroom team meetings. It was an opportunity for each team to work on their agenda.

Staff Participation in Decision Making

Allowing staff to participate in the decisions made in your program is an important piece in providing a program where employees will want to stay. Employees cannot make all the decisions, of course, but they can be informed about your decision-making process, or about the decisions that are being made and by whom they are being made. Chapter 7 explores this topic in detail. After all, most of these decisions will directly affect the working conditions of the employees.

REFERENCES

Bloom, P. J., Sheerer, M., & Britz, J. (1991). *Blueprint for Action: Achieving center-based change through staff development*. Lake Forest, IL: New Horizons Press. Reprinted with permission. All rights reserved.

Center for the Child Care Workforce. (1998). *Creating better child care jobs: Model work standards for teaching staff in center-based child care*. Washington, DC: Center for the Child Care Workforce.

Center for the Child Care Workforce. (2001, March). *Current data on child care salaries and benefits in the United States*. Washington, DC: Center for the Child Care Workforce.

Delps, A., & Guerin, L. (2001). *Dealing with Problem Employees: A Legal Guide*. Berkeley, CA: Nolo Press.

Early Childhood Directors Association. (1990). *Policies and Procedures for Early Childhood Directors*. St. Paul, MN: Toys 'N Things Press.

Foumies, F. F. (1999). *Why Employees Don't Do What They're Supposed To Do*. New York: McGraw-Hill.

Kaplan, V., & Kunreuther, R. (1996). *The A-to-Z Guide of Managing People*. New York: Berkeley Books.

HELPFUL WEB SITES

http://www.ccw.org
The Center for the Child Care Workforce.

http://www.bls.gov/oco
Web site for the U.S. Department of Labor's wage data.

http://www.employeehandbookstore.com
http://www.sampleemployeehandbook.com
Two Web sites that offer software for preparing employee handbooks.

The Budget

For many early childhood administrators, preparing the budget is the most difficult and least enjoyable part of their job. Yet, as the administrator, you are responsible for this most important document. It is often one of the yardsticks against which you will be measured, so it is important that you master certain simple techniques in order to compile your budget and then, once you have a completed, approved document, use it as a planning tool. A sound budget, well used, can also move your program in the direction you have envisioned, while helping you maintain the financial integrity of your organization.

THE BASIC BUDGET

What exactly is a budget and why is it such an important tool? A budget for your organization is exactly the same thing as your personal budget. It allows you to plan how you will spend money in the coming **fiscal** (or accounting) **period** and tells you the amount of income you are expecting to collect. Your fiscal year is whatever you have defined as the 12-month period that is your accounting year, whether January through December, July through June, or some other 12-month period. Your budget allows you to plan your strategy for making money in the fiscal year ahead, or at least spending only as much as you anticipate collecting (called a **break-even budget**). It helps you measure your activity during the year to determine whether you are operating on track and helps you know beforehand whether you will end the year without losing money. A good budget provides the information needed to make the necessary changes to your operations if required during the course of the year. You can initially create only one budget, or you can create several different budgets, each based on different assumptions. Only one budget will ultimately be selected as the one you will use and against which you will track your actual income and expenses.

In its most basic form, an annual budget for a child care program in which you assume 100 percent enrollment for every month of the year might look something like this:

Income (revenue)	$100,000.00
Expenses	$85,000.00
Net surplus or (deficit)*	$15,000.00

(*In a for-profit enterprise, this bottom-line result is the same thing as your profit or loss.)

If you assume, on the other hand, only 80 percent enrollment, with the same level of expenses, your budget might look like this:

Income (revenue)	$80,000.00
Expenses	$85,000.00
Net surplus or (deficit)	($ 5,000.00)

Or, you could forecast 80 percent enrollment, but assume you will spend less in expenses:

Income (revenue)	$80,000.00
Expenses	$78,000.00
Net surplus or (deficit)	$ 2,000.00

Once you have established your budget for the year, it *does not change*. If you spend more or less than planned in your budget, or you earn more or less than the budgeted revenue, these are **variances,** or differences, from your budget and reflect circumstances that occurred during the year that you probably did not anticipate. These variances actually help you see where your program has deviated from the plan (your budget) and guide you toward ways to get you back on plan.

As a blueprint for what revenues and expenses are anticipated for the year ahead, the budget becomes a tool by which you measure how well your organization is doing financially. (See Chapter 5 for a complete discussion of using your budget as a planning tool.) By tracking what you actually spend and what you actually receive in revenue every month in comparison to what you have budgeted to spend and receive, you can immediately see where your actual costs and revenues differ (or vary) from what you had planned. Knowing these variances before the end of the year, especially if they affect your program in a negative way, will help you plan ways to reduce the adverse effects. Then, if you need to make some adjustments in, say, spending, to compensate for an unanticipated drop in revenue, you are able to do so as soon as you recognize there is a problem. Without a budget to follow, you are left to guess at how well you are doing, and you will probably not know whether you made or lost money until the accountant prepares your year-end tax return or your bank account is depleted.

A budget usually covers one year but you may want to plan budgets for two, three, or five years in the future. The further into the future you plan, however, the harder it is to estimate accurately how your program will evolve. Multiyear budgets can be used to give you the bigger picture for your program. You can plan how your program will expand over the next five years, for example, or how you plan to raise compensation for all employees, or build an addition to your center.

Once you have an approved budget, it can be broken down into monthly, quarterly, or semiannual budgets by dividing the annual figures by 12, 4, or 2, respectively. Thus in its most simple form, a budget for one month in a center whose annual budget is the first one

! TIP

Using a monthly budget enables you to monitor your income and expenses throughout the year.

described above would be:

Income per month	$8,333.33	(or $100,000/12)
Expenses per month	$7,083.33	(or $85,000/12)
Net surplus/month	$1,250.00	

EXPENSE COMPONENTS

In constructing a budget, I recommend working on the expense side first and "backing into" the revenue figures. This means that you first estimate what your costs will be for the year according to the decisions you make about your center's program, then determine how much revenue you need to just cover those costs (again, that's our break-even budget) or make a small surplus. Now, I am not suggesting you have unlimited flexibility in deciding what your fees will be. By first gauging your expenses, it will help you aim toward the most appropriate fee schedule. However, if your revenue is constrained in some way by agencies or individuals you do not control, or if you are the owner of a small home child care business, you may need to start with what your revenue is expected to be. These figures will place a limit on how much you can spend.

✓ Hint

Start your budget planning with an estimate of your expenses. Then determine what level of income you must have to cover these costs.

I typically run three different budget scenarios: one "reasonable" estimate of what I think will happen, one "blue sky" budget that allows me to dream if earnings reflect full enrollment most of the year, and one "conservative" budget that anticipates seasonally low enrollment or cuts in funding and/or grants and looks at more of a worst-case possibility. Building several budget scenarios allows you to understand the choices open to you and the trade-offs made when deciding how much to spend and where to spend it. For example, by raising tuition by 5 percent instead of 4 percent, how much more money is generated over the course of the year, and what will that additional revenue pay for? Will it be used to reimburse teachers for their expenses attending the state conference? Will the additional revenue be used to bring in on-site trainers for our staff? Will it be used to buy the new washer and dryer you know will be needed sometime during the year?

Looking at more than one budget scenario helps you to anticipate what actions you may need to take in the event of a decline in your revenues. If your board (corporation, supervisor) does not approve a tuition increase for the coming year, how are you going to raise teacher salaries? How are you going to hire that fabulous mentor teacher for the pre-K room? How are you going to pay for the 75 percent increase you anticipate in your worker's compensation premium? These are discussions you want to have *before* you are faced with a financial crisis.

Expense Line Items in Your Budget

By starting with expenses, you can determine what level of revenue you must obtain in order to cover your costs of doing business. Some components that are common expenses in a child care program include:

staff salaries

staff benefits

rent

janitorial services

insurance

legal and professional fees

maintenance

supplies (for the classrooms, office, and general cleaning)

utilities

Some of these expense components, such as insurance (liability insurance, accident insurance, etc.) and rent costs are **fixed costs.** That is, these costs are prescribed to you by an outside agency and the amount of these costs does not change with the number of families served or staff employed. These costs are the easiest to estimate. For example, you can usually determine ahead of time, by talking with your insurance company or broker, approximately how much of an increase there will be in the costs of insurance premiums. Find a company or broker you feel you can trust and expect her to find you the lowest cost policy with the best coverage. Typically, a child care program will need the following kinds of insurance:

- *general liability policy* to cover losses due to fire, theft, or someone suing you
- *accident insurance* to cover the cost of medical care for the children in your program who are hurt at school
- *fidelity bond* to cover your losses if one of your employees steals from you
- *directors and officers liability insurance* to protect senior management in the event that they are sued, either by a parent or, more typically, by a former employee

Your insurance costs may be increasing by 12 percent. On the other hand, you have been told that there will only be a 5 percent increase in rent for the following year.

Another fixed cost you will estimate is that of legal and professional fees. This category includes such items as hiring a certified public accountant (CPA) to complete your tax returns annually or perform an accounting audit, retaining legal advice, or perhaps paying for a consultant or bookkeeper who is not an employee.

Maintenance, though usually a small budget expense, should also be estimated. This category includes plumbing repairs, roof repairs, etc., and the cost of repairing the washing machine, dishwasher, or copying machine when they are broken. *Utilities* include all the costs of telephone, water, heating, electricity, and waste disposal. Again, although these costs go up and down through the year, they are fixed in the sense that an outside vendor is setting the prices *and* these costs essentially do not vary when the number of children in your program changes.

Costs that are not fixed are **variable costs.** These are costs that *vary* depending on the volume of your program, i.e., the number of children enrolled, the number of classrooms, or the number of teachers employed. These costs are much harder to estimate, since they can change based on the assumptions you make about staffing and enrollment. Every time you consider adding a teacher, or adding additional students in your program, these costs will increase. These costs are usually within your control; an administrator will usually have some discretion about or at least be part of the process of deciding whether more teachers are hired, what their hours will be, if some teachers are laid off, or if students are added to the program.

Step One in Building Your Budget: Estimating Current Year's Total Expenses

The best way to assess all your costs is to start with what you have spent in the past, then estimate how much each line item expense will increase in the year to come. (Costs seldom decrease!) This is one reason why it is important to keep complete and accurate financial records: not only does it show you what you have spent, but it helps in estimating what future costs will be.

As a starting point for the estimation of the expenses for the budget year, step one in building your budget is to estimate your *current* year's total revenues and expenses. If you are starting to build next year's budget some months before the end of your current year (which we *always* want to do), you may not have a full 12 months of operating results. We must first estimate what we think the total of this year's revenue and expenses will be. In order to estimate the total current year's costs you can use

a) the most recent past month for which you have complete data to estimate "typical" monthly expenses for the remaining months of the year;

b) the most recent two (or three or four) months to estimate the remaining two (or three or four) months of the year;

c) the average of the data from the past months of the current year for which you have complete data as an estimate for the remaining months of the year; or

d) the last three (or however many months left in your current year) months' *budget* figures added on to the nine months' *actual* figures.

In Figure 4–1, an estimate has been made of the full current year for the Felton Family Preschool from actual results for the first nine months, September through May, by using

Felton Family Preschool
Estimating Current Year's Financial Results

	Sept. 1–May 31 Current Year Results(9 Mos.)	Avg. Month Current Year	Estimate 3 More Months	Estimated Current Year Results(Full Year)
INCOME				
Tuition	236,250	26,250	78,750	315,000
Fund-raising	5,250	583	1,750	7,000
County Grant	15,000	1,667	5,000	20,000
Other	1,500	167	500	2,000
TOTAL INCOME	258,000	28,667	86,000	344,000
EXPENSE				
Payroll Expense				
Salaries-Staff	185,420	20,602	61,807	247,227
Payroll Taxes	16,688	1,854	5,563	22,250
Worker's Comp	7,417	824	2,472	9,889
Staff Benefits				
Health Ins.	18,750	2,083	6,250	25,000
Dental Ins.	3,000	333	1,000	4,000
Education Allow.	656	73	219	875
Rent	3,600	400	1,200	4,800
Janitor	4,500	500	1,500	6,000
Insurance				
Accident	1,125	125	375	1,500
Directors Ins.	674	75	225	899
Liability	2,081	231	694	2,775
Supplies	10,540	1,171	3,513	14,053
Utilities	2,025	225	675	2,700
Capital Improvement	0	0	0	0
TOTAL EXPENSES	256,476	28,497	85,492	341,968
SURPLUS (DEFICIT)	1,524	169	508	2,032

FIGURE 4–1 Estimating Current Year's Financial Results for Felton Family Preschool

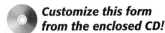

Customize this form from the enclosed CD!

method (c), just described: the average of the actual nine months for which we have data. Column D tells us what the total revenue and expenses have been for these nine months. In the column labeled "Avg. Month Current Year," the figures from Column D have been divided by nine to calculate an "average" month. These numbers tell us that even though there have been ups and downs in our budget all year, *on average* this figure represents a good estimate of a monthly expense.

The averages from Column E are multiplied by three in Column F, labeled "Estimate 3 More Months," to give us the total figure for our estimate for the months of June, July, and August. By adding the figures in Column F to the figures in Column D, we arrive at our final estimate for the current year in Column G, "Estimated Current Year Results."

Step Two in Building Your Budget: Estimating Future Budget Expenses

Step two in building your budget is to estimate what you expect expenses to be in the *budget* year by multiplying the estimate of a *current* annual expense by either a percent increase or a percent decrease.

1. You can use the same percentage for each expense line item.
2. You can use different percentages for different line items depending upon your expectations.
3. You can use the specific information you have collected for your fixed costs.

Start-up and Home Child Care Budgets

I f you are running a home child care business, or are just starting out to plan a new center, you will often not have any "current" operating statistics. You have nothing to use as a base for estimating the future. In these cases you will be using a different approach for establishing your expense budget.

Starting from the *revenue* side, describe what your enrollment and staffing will look like, as we did in Chapter 2. How many children, what ages, and what schedules will you accommodate? From this scenario, you will be able to estimate what your costs will be in each of the categories. It's that simple. If your program will be hiring teachers and/or administrative staff, you will probably need to construct a separate salary spreadsheet. Determine work schedules and rates of pay based on the needs of your program and information you have collected in your community concerning prevailing wage rates. Don't forget to add in your own compensation, even if you are a one-person business. Add in an amount of money that you believe is a reasonable annual salary. If you operate out of your home as a sole proprietor (meaning you are not

incorporated as a business or partnership), your salary will be whatever is left over after all your other expenses are paid. However, in order to plan your business so that you are actually earning a living, you should act as if you are your own employee.

Add in costs for insurance you will need and the costs of payroll taxes. You will need at least a general liability policy and a child accident insurance policy. Insurance costs can be determined by talking with an insurance broker if you are just starting a program, or reviewing what policies you now have and how much they cost. Finding an insurance broker can be helpful and will ensure that you are adequately covered.

When you have compiled all costs and have a total annual expense budget, you know what you need to earn each year to cover those costs. A sample budget for a home child care business is shown in Figure 4–2. A discussion of tuition fee rate setting can be found in Chapter 2. In subsequent years, you will have past and current information from which to develop new budgets and can use any of the methods described in this text.

continues

Start-up and Home Child Care Budgets *continued*

	A	B	C	D	E	F	G
1							
2			**Sallie's Home Care**				
3							
4						Annual	
5						Budget	
6		INCOME					
7		Tuition				$54,120	
8		Fund-raising				$0	
9		Other					
10							
11							
12		TOTAL INCOME				$54,120	
13							
14		EXPENSE					
15		Payroll Expense					
16		Salaries-Staff	(salary of $28,000 + one employee)			$42,000	
17		Payroll Taxes				$3,780	
18		Worker's Comp				$2,100	
19							
20		Staff Benefits					
21		Health Ins.				$0	
22		Dental Ins.				$0	
23							
24		Insurance					
25		Accident				$400	
26		Liability				$500	
27							
28		Supplies				$1,000	
29							
30		Maintenance				$500	
31							
32		Utilities				$600	
33							
34		Capital Improvement				$1,000	
35							
36		TOTAL EXPENSES				$51,880	
37							
38		SURPLUS (DEFICIT)				$2,240	
39							

FIGURE 4–2 Sample Budget for Sallie's Home Care

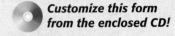

Customize this form from the enclosed CD!

Thus, if you expect the rent, which was $4,800 in the current year, to increase by 5 percent,

multiply $4,800 by 1 plus .05

(4800 × 1.05) which equals $5,040.

Working with Spreadsheets. A spreadsheet like the one depicted in Figure 4–3 allows you to display and change percent increases or decreases to see the effect on the total of

		Estimated Current Year Results (12 Mos)	"Reasonable" Budget A	"Blue Sky" Budget B	"Conservative" Budget C	Percentage Change
Felton Family Preschool						
Three Sample Expense Budgets						
INCOME						
Tuition		315,000				0.02
Fund-raising		7,000				0.03
County Grant		20,000				0.04
Other		2,000				0.05
						0.06
TOTAL INCOME		344,000				0.09
						0.1
EXPENSE						0.15
Payroll Expense						0.2
Salaries-Staff		247,227	270,000	275,000	247,227	0.25
Payroll Taxes		22,250	24,300	24,750	22,250	
Worker's Comp		9,889	13,500	13,750	9,889	
Staff Benefits						
Health Ins.		25,000	27,250	27,500	26,500	
Dental Ins.		4,000	4,000	4,120	4,120	
Education Allow.		875	875	875	875	
Rent		4,800	4,800	4,800	4,800	
Janitor		6,000	6,000	6,000	6,000	
Insurance						
Accident		1,500	1,575	1,575	1,575	
Directors Ins.		899	944	944	944	
Liability		2,775	2,914	2,914	2,775	
Supplies		14,053	17,566	17,566	11,242	
Utilities		2,700	2,835	2,835	2,835	
Capital Improvement		0	5,000	7,000	0	
TOTAL EXPENSES		341,968	381,559	389,629	341,033	
SURPLUS (DEFICIT)		2,032				

FIGURE 4–3 Three Sample Expense Budgets for Felton Family Preschool

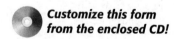

Customize this form from the enclosed CD!

expenses. It also allows you easily to prepare more than one budget plan based on your most optimistic, or most conservative, estimate of costs, and to work easily with different percentages from one line item to the next.

Learning and using computer spreadsheet software can be a tremendous assistance to the child care administrator. Although all of the budget preparation and analysis we are discussing can be done by hand, you will be able to save yourself a lot of time by using a computer. You will also have greater accuracy in the computations you do and greater flexibility in running repeated calculations based on different assumptions. One class in learning spreadsheet software such as Excel® will be sufficient to get you started in its use. Then the more you use it, the more proficient you will become. Appendix B contains a short discussion of the spreadsheet terminology we will be using in the following discussion.

Working with a Budget Spreadsheet. In Figure 4–3, in the column labeled "Estimated Current Year Results." we see the estimates we derived of the current year's totals. Columns E through G display three *different* expense scenarios based on different assumptions made for salary and benefit increases, insurance costs, capital improvements, etc. These budgets are listed below:

1. Budget A, a middle-of-the-road, "reasonable" budget
2. Budget B, the "blue sky" budget
3. Budget C, the most "conservative" budget

Because the spreadsheet calculates the totals, it is possible to vary the numbers in each column to see immediate results. Except for staff salaries, payroll taxes, worker's compensation, and the **cells** that contain subtotals, each cell in the spreadsheet is a fixed number or contains a formula that calculates the value in it as a percentage increase from the "Current Year Results" column. Staff salaries have been entered as a fixed number. Staff salaries are computed in a supporting worksheet that is discussed in the sections below.

Staff Salaries and Benefits.   Looking at the list of expenses, it is easy to see that the largest component on the expense side in a child care program is staff salaries and benefits. This will always be the case. On average, staffing costs (salaries, taxes, and benefits) comprise between 75 percent and 95 percent of a typical program's annual expenses. In our Budget A, staff salaries and benefits comprise 91 percent of all expenses.

Salaries	=	$270,000
Payroll taxes	+	$ 24,300
Worker's comp	+	$ 13,500
Health ins.	+	$ 27,250
Dental ins.	+	$ 4,000
Education	+	$ 875
Total	=	$339,925
$339,925/ $381,559	=	91%

! TIP

It hardly matters if you make errors in estimating costs other than salaries and benefits.

For this reason, staffing costs will always be the *most important* part of your budget on the cost side. Most of your effort in estimating costs, and controlling costs during the year, should be devoted to making as accurate an estimate as possible as to what it will cost to pay your teachers and other staff and what it will cost to pay for their benefits.

An error of 20 percent in, for example, the costs of office supplies for a year, will probably only amount to spending over your budget by less than $500 for the entire year. In comparison, an error of only 3 percent in estimating staff costs, in a program that spends $300,000 a year in staff salaries and benefits, would equal spending $9,000 more than you had budgeted—a much more significant error.

Wages paid to staff can be estimated in several ways, depending upon the size of your center, the number of staff employed, and the degree to which you may be planning to downsize or expand your center in the coming year. Most simply, staff wages in the new budget can be estimated by applying a percentage increase or decrease to the estimate of the current year's salary expense. This method is the most simple and works quite adequately for many small programs and home child care businesses.

Step Three in Building Your Budget: Constructing a Salary Spreadsheet

If you have a large program, or if you are considering making significant changes to staffing in the new year, it is a good idea to construct a separate worksheet that details staff costs. The total from this worksheet can transfer to the staff salaries line item on your budget

	Employee	Current Wage Rate	Budget Wage Rate	Hours/Wk	Annual Salary	
	Felton Family Preschool					
	Staff Salaries					
		Current	Budget		Annual	
	Employee	**Wage Rate**	**Wage Rate**	**Hours/Wk**	**Salary**	
	Latifa	$11.00	$12.00	40	$24,960	
	Sheena	$9.50	$10.00	30	$15,600	
	Carol	$8.00	$9.00	40	$18,720	
	Jean-Claude	$10.50	$11.00	35	$20,020	
	Marta	$10.00	$10.50	20	$10,920	
					$90,220	Total Toddler Staff
	Francis	$9.00	$10.00	40	$20,800	
	Georgia	$9.00	$9.50	30	$14,820	
	Janisha	$11.00	$11.50	30	$17,940	
	Juan	$11.00	$12.00	40	$24,960	
					$78,520	Total Young Preschool
	Dtr/Teacher	$12.00	$13.00	10	$6,760	
	Isabel	$10.00	$11.00	40	$22,880	
	Jodie	$9.75	$10.50	35	$19,110	
	Linda	$8.00	$9.00	40	$18,720	
					$67,470	Total Pre-K Staff
	Dtr/Teacher	$12.00	$13.00	30	$20,280	
	Substitutes				$13,510	
					$270,000	TOTAL SALARIES

FIGURE 4–4 Felton Family Preschool Staff Salaries

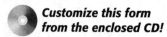

Customize this form from the enclosed CD!

worksheet. See the staff salaries spreadsheet for the Felton Preschool (Figure 4–4). If you have not already made an estimate of staff salaries as part of the estimation of budget expenses in step two, the construction of a separate salary spreadsheet is step three in our budget-building process.

Listed in the spreadsheet are each staff member, their current hourly wage, their projected (or budgeted) hourly wage, the number of hours they work per week, and the annual salary this wage rate equals. Column F, "Annual Salary" contains formulas that calculate the staff member's annual salary from the wage rate and their hours worked per week.

A teacher working 8 hours per day, 5 days per week, 52 weeks per year, works 2,080 hours in one year (8 × 5 × 52). The annual work hours of an employee working any less than an 8-hour day can be computed in a similar fashion. For example, a 6-hour shift would be

6 hrs/day × 5 days/wk × 52 wks/yr = 1,560 hrs/yr;

or someone working 3 days a week for 5 hours a day would work

5 hrs/day × 3 days/wk × 52 wks/yr = 780 hrs/yr.

Felton Family Preschool
Three Sample Expense Budgets

		Estimated Current Year Results(12 Mos)	"Reasonable" Budget A	"Blue Sky" Budget B	"Conservative" Budget C	Percentage Change
INCOME						
	Tuition	315,000				0.02
	Fund-raising	7,000				0.03
	County Grant	20,000				0.04
	Other	2,000				0.05
						0.06
	TOTAL INCOME	344,000				0.09
						0.1
						0.15
EXPENSE						0.2
	Payroll Expense					0.25
	Salaries-Staff	247,227	270,000	275,000	247,227	
	Payroll Taxes	22,250	24,300	24,750	22,250	
	Worker's Comp	9,889	13,500	13,750	9,889	
	Staff Benefits					
	Health Ins.	25,000	27,250	27,500	26,500	
	Dental Ins.	4,000	4,000	4,120	4,120	
	Education Allow.	875	875	875	875	
	Rent	4,800	4,800	4,800	4,800	
	Janitor	6,000	6,000	6,000	6,000	
	Insurance					
	Accident	1,500	1,575	1,575	1,575	
	Directors Ins.	899	944	944	944	
	Liability	2,775	2,914	2,914	2,775	
	Supplies	14,053	17,566	17,566	11,242	
	Utilities	2,700	2,835	2,835	2,835	
	Capital Improvement	0	5,000	7,000	0	
	TOTAL EXPENSES	341,968	381,559	389,629	341,033	
	SURPLUS (DEFICIT)	2,032				

FIGURE 4–5 Felton Family Preschool Three Sample Expense Budgets

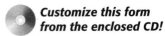

***Customize this form
from the enclosed CD!***

Thus, the formula for the annual salary of Latifa in the toddler program, which is hidden in Column F, is:

wage rate in Cell D8 × hrs/wk in Cell E8 × 52 wks/yr

$$D8 \times E8 \times 52 = \$24{,}960$$

This method includes all holidays and any sick or vacation days for which the teacher is paid. This formula calculates the *maximum* amount the employee will be paid in a year unless you pay bonuses to your staff and/or expect to pay them overtime wages. It is also usually the maximum amount that position will cost even if the starting teacher resigns. If the teacher resigns midyear and the position is unfilled for several weeks, you will still be paying someone, maybe a substitute teacher, to fill the position temporarily. This method of estimating the cost of employees includes any temporary staff you have to pay if a teacher resigns. However, it *does not include* the cost of a teacher brought in to replace the starting teacher at a *higher* wage rate partway through the year. It also *does not include* paying for a substitute when a teacher is using her paid vacation or sick time.

Felton Family Preschool
Staff Salaries

	Employee	Current Wage Rate	Budget Wage Rate	Hours/Wk	Annual Salary	
	Latifa	$11.00	$12.00	40	$24,960	
	Sheena	$9.50	$10.00	30	$15,600	
	Carol	$8.00	$9.00	40	$18,720	
	Jean-Claude	$10.50	$11.00	35	$20,020	
	Marta	$10.00	$10.50	20	$10,920	
					$90,220	Total Toddler Staff
	Francis	$9.00	$10.00	40	$20,800	
	Georgia	$9.00	$9.50	30	$14,820	
	Janisha	$11.00	$11.50	30	$17,940	
	Juan	$11.00	$12.00	40	$24,960	
					$78,520	Total Young Preschool
	Dtr/Teacher	$12.00	$13.00	10	$6,760	
	Isabel	$10.00	$11.00	40	$22,880	
	Jodie	$9.75	$10.50	35	$19,110	
	Linda	$8.00	$9.00	40	$18,720	
					$67,470	Total Pre-K Staff
	Dtr/Teacher	$12.00	$13.00	30	$20,280	
	Substitutes				$13,510	
					$270,000	TOTAL SALARIES

FIGURE 4–6 Felton Family Preschool Staff Salaries

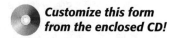

Customize this form from the enclosed CD!

If you know you use substitute teachers on a regular basis, you can either include a separate line in your budget for this cost or include the cost of substitutes with your regular employees. Based on what you have spent in the recent past on substitute salaries, you can estimate whether this expense will increase, decrease, or stay the same in the year ahead. If you do not have information from the past that separates out this cost for you, you may want to include a way to track this cost separately in the coming year. This may be a cost that can be contained if you find you need to cut expenses partway through the year.

Payroll taxes and worker's compensation insurance are calculated back in your budget spreadsheet as a percent of your center's total salaries. These state and federal taxes (Social Security, Medicare, unemployment, and disability) are approximately 9 percent of your salary line and should *always* be included when estimating the costs associated with your staff. Worker's comp costs are calculated from your particular insurance rates.

The first *budget* column in Figure 4–5, labeled "Reasonable," estimates the expense side of our budget including the total cost of salaries as computed in the salary spreadsheet, Figure 4–6.

We now have constructed a spreadsheet of three budget scenarios (Figure 4–5) with our cost estimates, and a spreadsheet for estimating staff salaries (Figure 4–6). The fourth step in completing the three budgets is an estimation of revenues (see discussion later in this chapter).

REVENUE COMPONENTS

There are usually several components that make up the total revenue of a child care program. The biggest line item is tuition fees paid by parents. Other types of revenue commonly seen for a child care program include:

registration fees

grants

fund-raising income

donations

food program revenue

state and/or federal funds

interest earned on cash savings

The most important element of keeping any program financially healthy is its enrollment. Any program can at the very least break even when the program is fully enrolled. If the key to valuable property is *location, location, location*, in child care the key to financial viability is *enrollment, enrollment, enrollment.*

Most of your time and effort in constructing the revenue side of a budget should go into making as accurate an estimate of tuition revenue as possible. The other sources of income for your program are either fixed or can be estimated from past experience. County, state, and/or federal funding as well as grant income should be fairly well known amounts, as is funding for your food program. Although you may not know these amounts exactly, there is usually someone you can call who can tell you their expectation of what your level of funding will be.

You may or may not want to include fund-raising income in your budgeted revenue. Since this is never money you can be sure of receiving, it is called **soft money.** The amount of money your organization can raise depends on the success of your fund-raisers, who typically are parents and staff. If you do include an amount for fund-raising revenue in your budget, you should use a very conservative figure that you are confident can be raised; i.e., an amount that has been successfully raised in the past.

Step Four in Building Your Budget: Estimating Tuition Revenue

The quickest and easiest way to estimate future revenues from tuition is to extrapolate from your past history as we have done with expenses. All this means is what you received in tuition revenue in the past is your best guess as to what your revenue will be in the future.

You can apply a percentage change to last year's total revenue for changes in your program that you anticipate. For example, if you expect to add 5 more preschool spaces for next year and last year you had a total of 50 full-time spaces, you will be adding 10 percent (5 divided by 50) more capacity. Then, assuming you do not change the fees you charge, you can expect your total revenue to increase by 10 percent over what it was last year. This gives you a *very rough* estimate of tuition revenue, since it assumes that your enrollment in the other 50 spaces is exactly what it was last year and that tuition rates are the same for all children. Or, if you expect to raise all tuition fees by 5 percent, and are not adding to capacity, then you can roughly estimate that your total tuition revenue will increase by 5 percent over last year's total.

If you are just starting up a program you will need to determine what your fees will be without the benefit of having a past from which to extrapolate. There is a full description of this process in Chapter 2.

It is advisable to get a more accurate estimate of your expected revenue since this number is the key to your program staying financially healthy. By using a spreadsheet (tailored to your individual program) in which you are able to change enrollment percentages and tuition rates, you will be able to calculate easily the total change in your revenue. A spreadsheet allows you to test different changes in your fee structure and see the results immediately.

Working with a Tuition Spreadsheet.   With the variability in services offered by child care programs, it is difficult to give you the one model to use for estimating tuition revenue. The spreadsheet examples to follow are just three of the very many variations that can be developed. They all derive from the same principles. The basic method is the same in all

Tips on Estimating Tuition Revenue

1) Using current year's total, apply a percent change:

   Current year total tuition revenue = $100,000.
   You are adding 5 more preschool spaces and no increase in tuition rates.
   Last year you had 50 spaces.
   You are adding 10 percent more spaces (5/50 = .10).
   Thus, you can expect 10 percent more revenue.
   Estimate of future tuition revenue = $100,000 + 10% of $100,000 = $110,000.
   OR, you are not adding any spaces, but are raising fees by 5 percent.
   Estimate of future tuition revenue = $100,000 + 5% of $100,000 = $105,000.

   OR

2) Construct a spreadsheet to forecast revenue
   Necessary for larger programs.
   Allows you to test numerous changes to your rate structure and immediately see the results.

Tips for Working with a Tuition Spreadsheet

Any spreadsheet should contain the following components:

1) ability to calculate tuition revenue based on varying assumptions about tuition rates and enrollment
2) enrollment estimates based on percentages of your program's licensed capacity
3) enrollment numbers grouped by the same-price category

	A	B	C	D	E	F	G	H	I
1									
2			**Felton Family Preschool**						
3			**Tuition Revenue Estimate**					0.04	
4									
5					Percent	Current	New		
6		Age of Child	Schedule	Capacity	Enrollment	Tuition Rate	Tuition Rate	Revenue/Month	
7									
8		18–30 Months	full-time	7	0.85	$750	$780	$4,641	
9			full-time:reduced rate	5	0.90	$550	$572	$2,574	
10			half-time	3	0.85	$450	$468	$1,193	
11			half-time:reduced rate	1	0.85	$340	$354	$301	
12			3 days/week	1	0.85	$550	$572	$486	
13			3-day:reduced rate	1	0.80	$425	$442	$354	
14									
15									
16		30–42 Months	full-time	8	0.90	$650	$676	$4,867	
17			full-time:reduced rate	4	0.90	$480	$499	$1,797	
18			half-time	4	0.85	$400	$416	$1,414	
19			half-time:reduced rate	2	0.90	$300	$312	$562	
20			3 days/week	1	0.85	$475	$494	$420	
21			3-day:reduced rate	1	0.80	$370	$385	$308	
22									
23									
24		42 Months +	full-time	8	0.90	$500	$520	$3,744	
25			full-time:reduced rate	4	0.90	$370	$385	$1,385	
26			half-time	4	0.80	$300	$312	$998	
27			half-time:reduced rate	4	0.90	$230	$239	$861	
28			3 days/week	4	0.85	$370	$385	$1,308	
29			3-day:reduced rate	2	0.80	$280	$291	$466	
30									
31									
32							Total/Month	$27,680	
33							Total/Year	$332,158	
34									

FIGURE 4–7 Felton Family Preschool Tuition Revenue Estimate

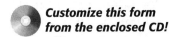

Customize this form from the enclosed CD!

examples and has the following components no matter how the particulars of your model may differ:

1. The model has the ability to calculate tuition revenue based on varying assumptions about tuition rates and enrollment.

2. Enrollment estimates are based on a percentage of your center's licensed capacity.

3. Enrollment numbers are grouped by the same-priced category, whether it is by children's ages, or sliding fees based on family income.

An example of a spreadsheet for calculating tuition revenue for the Felton Family Preschool appears in Figure 4–7. This program serves children from 18 months to 5-years-old in three classrooms. The program offers full-time and part-time schedules for families paying full tuition and families paying a reduced rate based on their income. The first two columns of the spreadsheet describe the age groups served and the schedules offered within each age group. The column labeled "Capacity" details the number of children you can serve for each of those schedules within an age group. The total of all children served is equal to your licensed capacity. Column F, "Current Tuition Rate," lists the program's current monthly tuition rates for each schedule and age group.

Column E ("Percent Enrollment") contains your estimate of the percent enrollment you are expecting for each category of service. A conservative estimate of 80 percent enrollment on all lines could be entered or an optimistic estimate of 100 percent enrollment, or something in between. Different percentages of enrollment can be entered for different programs and different age groups, as has been done here. An 85 percent enrollment for full-time toddlers where you can serve 7 children at full capacity means that you are expecting 85 percent of 7 (.85 × 7) or 5.95 full-time toddlers *on average*. Some months you may only have 5 children; some months you may have 6 or 7 children. If you estimate your enrollment will be at 100 percent, you are saying that for every day your program offers care, you will have 7 (7 × 1.00 = 7) full-time toddlers enrolled.

Column G ("New Tuition Rate") is the other column in which you can change numbers and try out different tuition increases or decreases to see the effect on total income. You can estimate percent increases (or decreases) from the current rates (Column F) to see the effect on total revenue. For purposes of simplicity, the formulas in Column G in this worksheet all assume an increase of 4 percent in tuition rates.

old tuition rate × 1.04 = new tuition rate

This spreadsheet will calculate the expected revenue per month in Column H for each service, then total for the whole program. The total monthly revenue is multiplied by 12 to determine the year's expected income from tuition at the bottom of the worksheet.

Figure 4–8 shows a layout for estimating tuition revenue for Sallie's Home Care. Figure 4–9 is a spreadsheet for a program that serves infants through preschool, does not offer a reduced rate service, and only serves full-time children.

Sallie's Home Care
Tuition Revenue Estimate

Age of Child	Schedule	Capacity	Percent Enrollment	New Tuition Rate	Revenue/Month
4–12 Months	full-time	2	0.80	$800	$1,280
13–24 Months	full-time	2	0.80	$800	$1,280
25 Months +	full-time	2	0.80	$800	$1,280
	half-time	3	0.80	$450	$1,080
				Total/Month	$4,920
				Total/Year	$54,120

FIGURE 4–8 Sallie's Home Care Tuition Revenue Estimate

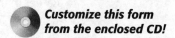

Customize this form from the enclosed CD!

Tuition Revenue Estimate

	Enrollment % =	0.95
	Tuition % =	0.04

Age of Child	Schedule	Capacity	Percent Enrollment	Current Tuition Rate	New Tuition Rate	Revenue/Month
2–24 Months	full-time	16	0.95	1000	1040	$15,808
	half-time					$0
	3 days/week					$0
	2 days/week					$0
	3 half days					$0
24–36 Months	full-time	24	0.95	800	832	$18,970
	half-time					$0
	3 days/week					$0
	2 days/week					$0
	3 half days					$0
36+ Months	full-time	40	0.95	700	728	$27,664
	half-time					$0
	3 days/week					$0
	2 days/week					$0
	3 half days					$0
					Total/Month	$62,442
					Total/Year	$749,299

FIGURE 4–9 Sample Tuition Revenue Forecasting Spreadsheet for Another Program

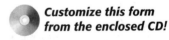

*Customize this form
from the enclosed CD!*

Step Five in Building Your Budget: Balancing the Budget

Once you are satisfied that you have developed a reasonable estimate of the revenue for the budget year, the total annual revenue figure is entered into the budget worksheet along with the projection of the year's expenses. Figure 4–10, which represents Step Five and the last step in the budget preparation process, depicts the first "round" of budget balancing for the Felton Family Preschool. The revenue and expense estimates we have just developed appear in Column E, labeled "Reasonable Budget A1."

Unfortunately, as you can see at the bottom of this column, these estimates result in a projected deficit for the year of $16,901:

	$364,658	total revenue
less	$381,559	total expenses
=	(16,901)	deficit

Rather than planning on losing money, your budget should be based on a small surplus for the year. Now is the time when the benefit of having these figures in a spreadsheet

	A	B	C	D	E	F
1						
2		**Felton Family Preschool**				
3		**First Pass Budget**				
4						
5				Estimated		
6				Current Year	"Reasonable"	
7				Results	Budget A1	
8		INCOME				
9		Tuition		315,000	332,158	
10		Fund-raising		7,000	3,500	
11		County Grant		20,000	27,000	
12		Other		2,000	2,000	
13						
14		TOTAL INCOME		344,000	364,658	
15						
16		EXPENSE				
17		Payroll Expense				
18		Salaries-Staff		247,227	270,000	
19		Payroll Taxes		22,250	24,300	
20		Worker's Comp		9,889	13,500	
21		Staff Benefits				
22		Health Ins.		25,000	27,250	
23		Dental Ins.		4,000	4,000	
24		Education Allow.		875	875	
25						
26		Rent		4,800	4,800	
27		Janitor		6,000	6,000	
28		Insurance				
29		Accident		1,500	1,575	
30		Directors Ins.		899	944	
31		Liability		2,775	2,914	
32		Supplies		14,053	17,566	
33		Utilities		2,700	2,835	
34						
35		Capital Improvement		0	5,000	
36						
37		TOTAL EXPENSES		341,968	381,559	
38						
39		SURPLUS (DEFICIT)		2,032	(16,901)	
40						

FIGURE 4–10 Felton Family Preschool First-Pass Budget

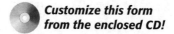

Customize this form from the enclosed CD!

becomes evident. We will be reworking the numbers, both expenses and revenues, until we can balance this budget and finalize figures we believe are very reasonable and which specify how the Felton Preschool will operate without losing money.

In Figure 4–11, Column F, labeled "Reasonable Budget A2," is our second pass in trying to balance this budget. We can either reduce expenses, raise revenue, or do a little of both, to bring our budget into balance. If we make adjustments to the cost side first, we could, for example, reduce the cost of supplies for the year by $2,566, to $15,000. Unfortunately, it looks like we will have to eliminate our capital improvement budget completely and hope we are able to raise money during the year for the capital projects we want to do. Most of the other expenses in our budget cannot be changed as easily. They are not only essential to our operations, but these expense amounts are for the most part fixed by outside agencies. Health insurance costs could be reduced. But because these

Felton Family Preschool
Balancing the Budget and Final Budget

		Estimated Current Year Results(12 Mos)	"Reasonable" Budget A1	"Reasonable" Budget A2	"Reasonable" Budget A3
INCOME					
	Tuition	315,000	332,158	332,158	**344,235**
	Fund-raising	7,000	3,500	3,500	3,500
	County Grant	20,000	27,000	27,000	27,000
	Other	2,000	2,000	2,000	2,000
	TOTAL INCOME	344,000	364,658	364,658	376,735
EXPENSE					
	Payroll Expense				
	Salaries-Staff	247,227	270,000	270,000	270,000
	Payroll Taxes	22,250	24,300	24,300	24,300
	Worker's Comp	9,889	13,500	13,500	13,500
	Staff Benefits				
	Health Ins.	25,000	27,250	27,250	27,250
	Dental Ins.	4,000	4,000	4,000	4,000
	Education Allow.	875	875	875	875
	Rent	4,800	4,800	4,800	4,800
	Janitor	6,000	6,000	6,000	6,000
	Insurance				
	Accident	1,500	1,575	1,575	1,575
	Directors Ins.	899	944	944	944
	Liability	2,775	2,914	2,914	2,914
	Supplies	14,053	17,566	**15,000**	15,000
	Utilities	2,700	2,835	2,835	2,835
	Capital Improvement		5,000	**0**	**2,000**
	TOTAL EXPENSES	341,968	381,559	373,993	375,993
	SURPLUS (DEFICIT)	2,032	(16,901)	(9,335)	742

FIGURE 4–11 Balancing the Budget and Final Budget for Felton Family Preschool

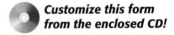

Customize this form from the enclosed CD!

rates are determined by the health insurance provider, we can only reduce this total line item by

a) reducing the benefits of the plan we offer staff,

b) increasing the portion of the premium paid by staff, or

c) finding a new insurance carrier with lower rates.

If you are reluctant to reduce any items affecting staff compensation and benefits, you must look to other variable costs in your budget and determine which of these can be trimmed.

After reducing the cost of supplies and eliminating our capital improvement budget, however, budget A2 is still not in balance. This revised budget produces a $9,335 deficit.

We may be tempted to accept budget A2 and hope that we are able to control costs in the coming year and that tuition revenue and fund-raising are as high as we have budgeted.

Going into a new year with a projected deficit or loss, however, is not recommended. It is better at this point to increase the revenue side of our budget and cut additional expenses to produce a small surplus (or "cushion") for the year, and thus we would be in a better position to absorb any unanticipated cost increases that might occur during the year.

The last column in our worksheet in Figure 4–11, labeled "Reasonable Budget A3," incorporates an adjustment in the "Tuition Revenue" line and a reinstatement of a small budget for capital improvements.

Revenue is increased by going back to the revenue estimating spreadsheet (Figure 4–7) and adjusting the tuition fees we will charge based on the work we did in Chapter 2. Our adjusted fee structure now more accurately reflects the full cost of care in our program and the rates charged by other comparable programs in our community. The computation for the revision of our revenue figures appears in Figure 4–12. Column G contains the newly revised tuition rates. Our assumptions about enrollment have not changed. The new total annual revenue figure is $344,235.

Felton Family Preschool
Tuition Revenue Estimate

	Age of Child	Schedule	Capacity	Percent Enrollment	Current Tuition Rate	New Tuition Rate	Revenue/Month
				Revised			
9	18–30 Months	full-time	7	0.85	$750	$825	$4,909
10		full-time:reduced rate	5	0.90	$550	$635	$2,858
11		half-time	3	0.85	$450	$450	$1,148
12		half-time:reduced rate	1	0.85	$340	$340	$289
13		3 days/week	1	0.85	$550	$600	$510
14		3-day:reduced rate	1	0.80	$425	$425	$340
17	30–42 Months	full-time	8	0.90	$650	$700	$5,040
18		full-time:reduced rate	4	0.90	$480	$480	$1,728
19		half-time	4	0.85	$400	$425	$1,445
20		half-time:reduced rate	2	0.90	$300	$300	$540
21		3 days/week	1	0.85	$475	$550	$468
22		3-day:reduced rate	1	0.80	$370	$400	$320
25	42 Months +	full-time	8	0.90	$500	$525	$3,780
26		full-time:reduced rate	4	0.90	$370	$400	$1,440
27		half-time	4	0.80	$300	$350	$1,120
28		half-time:reduced rate	4	0.90	$230	$230	$828
29		3 days/week	4	0.85	$370	$425	$1,445
30		3-day:reduced rate	2	0.80	$280	$300	$480
33						Total/Month	$28,686
34						Total/Year	$344,235

FIGURE 4–12 Revised Tuition Revenue Estimate for Felton Family Preschool Budget

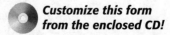

Customize this form from the enclosed CD!

Felton Family Preschool
Budget

		Estimated Current Year Results(12 Mos)	"Reasonable" Budget A1	"Reasonable" Budget A2	"Reasonable" Budget A3
INCOME					
	Tuition	315,000	332,158	332,158	**344,235**
	Fund-raising	7,000	3,500	3,500	3,500
	County Grant	20,000	27,000	27,000	27,000
	Other	2,000	2,000	2,000	2,000
TOTAL INCOME		344,000	364,658	364,658	376,735
EXPENSE					
	Payroll Expense				
	Salaries-Staff	247,227	270,000	270,000	270,000
	Payroll Taxes	22,250	24,300	24,300	24,300
	Worker's Comp	9,889	13,500	13,500	13,500
	Staff Benefits				
	Health Ins.	25,000	27,250	27,250	27,250
	Dental Ins.	4,000	4,000	4,000	4,000
	Education Allow.	875	875	875	875
	Rent	4,800	4,800	4,800	4,800
	Janitor	6,000	6,000	6,000	6,000
	Insurance				
	Accident	1,500	1,575	1,575	1,575
	Directors Ins.	899	944	944	944
	Liability	2,775	2,914	2,914	2,914
	Supplies	14,053	17,566	**15,000**	15,000
	Utilities	2,700	2,835	2,835	2,835
	Capital Improvement		5,000	**0**	**2,000**
TOTAL EXPENSES		341,968	381,559	373,993	375,993
SURPLUS (DEFICIT)		2,032	(16,901)	(9,335)	742

FIGURE 4–13 Felton Family Preschool Budget

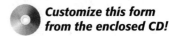

Customize this form from the enclosed CD!

Budget A3 in Figure 4–13 incorporates the new estimate of tuition revenue ($344,235) and the new amount for capital improvement ($2,000), and what was a bottom-line deficit in budget A2 ($9,335) has become a small surplus of $742 for the year.

The revision of expense and revenue items is often a multistep process, and could involve others on your staff, parents in your organization, or upper-level management. There are usually many solutions to balancing a budget, any one of which may be the best solution for your organization, or may be the only one that will gain approval from the other parties involved. The process, however, remains the same: adding to revenues, or taking from expenses, maybe even cutting revenues *and* costs, or some combination of these.

In the same manner, it is possible to construct and balance the "blue sky" budget and the "conservative" budget in order to present more than one alternative to your decision-making body. Presenting more than one alternative will inform all parties as to the trade-offs that must be made in order to increase, say, staff salaries, or to make allowances for capital improvements. It allows you to look at the conditions you may have to face if your enrollment is not as strong as you have experienced in the past.

WHAT NEXT?

Now that we have an approved budget, are we done? What do we do with it? Don't hide it in a drawer. Don't forget about it until next year's budget-planning time. All the time and energy poured into creating this document will pay off. This document becomes a planning tool for you to use throughout the budget year.

The Budget as a Planning Tool

USING YOUR BUDGET

Once your budget has been finalized, the budget and its supporting documents become your blueprint for the year ahead. They tell you what your enrollment goals are for each of the age levels and each of the schedules, and thus help guide your activities to enroll new families. The budget informs the fundraisers in your organization (maybe that's you, too!) as to how much money must be raised to meet budget targets. And the budget also specifies the amounts you are planning to spend in each of your cost categories. When you break down your annual budget into smaller pieces—for example, monthly budgets—this document guides you from month to month, documenting how well or how poorly you are doing financially. You measure how closely the program has met its enrollment goals and whether it has stayed within its spending limitations.

ESTIMATING MONTHLY BUDGET AMOUNTS

In order to use your budget as a planning tool most effectively, the annual budget is broken down into manageable pieces. Typically, an organization will track actual monthly revenues and expenses against monthly budgeted amounts. Figure 5–1 displays the annual budget (A3) for the Felton Family Preschool from Figure 4–13, Column G. In order to determine the monthly budget amounts, you can

divide the annual amounts by 12 for each monthly amount.

That is what has been done in Figure 5–1. Columns E through P show equal monthly budget amounts for each line item. Each monthly column represents one-twelfth of the

Felton Family Preschool

Monthly Budget

	"Reasonable" Budget A3	September	October	November	December	January	February	March	April	May	June	July	August
INCOME													
Tuition	344,235	28,686	28,686	28,686	28,686	28,686	28,686	28,686	28,686	28,686	28,686	28,686	28,686
Fund-raising	3,500	292	292	292	292	292	292	292	292	292	292	292	292
County Grant	27,000	2,250	2,250	2,250	2,250	2,250	2,250	2,250	2,250	2,250	2,250	2,250	2,250
Other	2,000	167	167	167	167	167	167	167	167	167	167	167	167
TOTAL INCOME	376,735	31,395	31,395	31,395	31,395	31,395	31,395	31,395	31,395	31,395	31,395	31,395	31,395
EXPENSE													
Payroll Expense													
Salaries-Staff	270,000	22,500	22,500	22,500	22,500	22,500	22,500	22,500	22,500	22,500	22,500	22,500	22,500
Payroll Taxes	24,300	2,025	2,025	2,025	2,025	2,025	2,025	2,025	2,025	2,025	2,025	2,025	2,025
Worker's Comp	13,500	1,125	1,125	1,125	1,125	1,125	1,125	1,125	1,125	1,125	1,125	1,125	1,125
Staff Benefits													
Health Ins.	27,250	2,271	2,271	2,271	2,271	2,271	2,271	2,271	2,271	2,271	2,271	2,271	2,271
Dental Ins.	4,000	333	333	333	333	333	333	333	333	333	333	333	333
Education Allow.	875	73	73	73	73	73	73	73	73	73	73	73	73
Rent	4,800	400	400	400	400	400	400	400	400	400	400	400	400
Janitor	6,000	500	500	500	500	500	500	500	500	500	500	500	500
Insurance													
Liability	2,914	243	243	243	243	243	243	243	243	243	243	243	243
Accident	1,575	131	131	131	131	131	131	131	131	131	131	131	131
Directors Ins.	944	79	79	79	79	79	79	79	79	79	79	79	79
Supplies	15,000	1,250	1,250	1,250	1,250	1,250	1,250	1,250	1,250	1,250	1,250	1,250	1,250
Utilities	2,835	236	236	236	236	236	236	236	236	236	236	236	236
Capital Improvement	2,000	167	167	167	167	167	167	167	167	167	167	167	167
TOTAL EXPENSES	375,993	31,333	31,333	31,333	31,333	31,333	31,333	31,333	31,333	31,333	31,333	31,333	31,333
SURPLUS (DEFICIT)	742	62	62	62	62	62	62	62	62	62	62	62	62

Customize this form from the enclosed CD!

FIGURE 5–1 Felton Family Preschool Monthly Budget

annual budget. It assumes you are spending and receiving the same amount of money in each line item category every month. It assumes the same enrollment every month and the same staff salary cost every month. Each month is projecting the same small surplus amount.

It is true that budgeting the same amounts each month is an oversimplification of what you expect to happen. However, it is a rough approximation of your *average* monthly expenses and revenue. It is not as accurate as using method number two described below, but it has the advantage of being quick and easy to set up. For many smaller programs, this is the method I recommend.

For home child care businesses, a one-twelfth division of income and expense, or some other simplified approach, makes the most sense. If you know you are closed, for example, for the month of August, then you can divide your budget *revenue* items evenly over the remaining 11 months, and, assuming your expenses continue whether your program is open or not, divide your *expense* items over all 12 months. Figure 5–2 illustrates a monthly budget allocation for Sallie's Home Care where she has evenly divided revenue over the 11 months of the year that her program is open, and expense over 12 months.

Alternatively, you can establish your monthly budget amounts based on past experience, by dividing some or all of the annual budget figures into amounts which are different each month.

For example, if you know that your program is usually not fully enrolled in the first months of its year (September, October) because you are bringing in new families to your program, then enrollment in those two months will be lower than in the rest of the year.

Figure 5–3 shows our same annual budget in the first column of figures, but some categories of income and expense are divided into unequal monthly budget amounts in the next 12 columns. Items such as rent are divided equally each month, since you know your rent does not change month to month. Capital improvement expense is unevenly divided, because you may be planning your capital purchases to occur in only two months of the year, November and March. The other items that have been unevenly distributed over the 12 months are tuition income and those expenses associated with payroll.

Estimating Salaries

✓Hint

Pay particular attention when estimating staffing costs, as these are always the largest expense in any child care budget.

When dividing your budget into uneven monthly figures, the two categories that require the most careful estimation because they are the largest categories in your budget, are salaries and tuition revenue. Salaries based on an hourly wage will actually vary month to month even when you are paying the same teachers the same wages, because there are a different number of hours and days paid each month. Whereas February in a particular year may only have 20 paid days, there may be 22 paid days in April. The April payroll will have two additional paid days in it. Other variances from month to month may occur when an employee works a different number of hours week to week, or when you have paid overtime to employees. All of these, and other, factors could cause your salary expense to vary by as much as 10 to 15 percent from one month to the next.

For these reasons you may want to estimate each month's salary expense as carefully as you can. The quickest and easiest way to do this is to count the number of paid days (including holidays, too, if staff receive pay for these days) in each pay period in the budget year. So, for example, if we assume the following:

September	22 paid days
October	23 paid days
November	20 paid days
December	23 paid days

Sallie's Home Care
Monthly Budget

	Annual Budget	September	October	November	December	January	February	March	April	May	June	July	Closed in August
INCOME													
Tuition	54,120	4,920	4,920	4,920	4,920	4,920	4,920	4,920	4,920	4,920	4,920	4,920	0
Fund-raising	0	0	0	0	0	0	0	0	0	0	0	0	0
TOTAL INCOME	54,120	4,920	4,920	4,920	4,920	4,920	4,920	4,920	4,920	4,920	4,920	4,920	0
EXPENSE													
Payroll Expense													
Salaries-Staff	42,000	3,500	3,500	3,500	3,500	3,500	3,500	3,500	3,500	3,500	3,500	3,500	3,500
Payroll Taxes	3,780	315	315	315	315	315	315	315	315	315	315	315	315
Worker's Comp	2,100	175	175	175	175	175	175	175	175	175	175	175	175
Insurance													
Liability	500	42	42	42	42	42	42	42	42	42	42	42	42
Accident	400	33	33	33	33	33	33	33	33	33	33	33	33
Supplies	1,000	83	83	83	83	83	83	83	83	83	83	83	83
Maintenance	500	42	42	42	42	42	42	42	42	42	42	42	42
Utilities	600	50	50	50	50	50	50	50	50	50	50	50	50
Capital Improvement	1,000	83	83	83	83	83	83	83	83	83	83	83	83
TOTAL EXPENSES	51,880	4,323	4,323	4,323	4,323	4,323	4,323	4,323	4,323	4,323	4,323	4,323	4,323
SURPLUS (DEFICIT)	2,240	4,920	597	597	597	597	597	597	597	597	597	597	(4,323)

FIGURE 5–2 Sallie's Home Care Monthly Budget

Customize this form from the enclosed CD!

Felton Family Preschool
Monthly Budget

	"Reasonable" Budget A3	September	October	November	December	January	February	March	April	May	June	July	August
INCOME													
Tuition	344,235	25,000	28,000	30,000	30,000	30,000	30,000	30,000	30,000	30,000	27,078	27,078	27,078
Fund-raising	3,500	292	292	292	292	292	292	292	292	292	292	292	292
County Grant	27,000	2,250	2,250	2,250	2,250	2,250	2,250	2,250	2,250	2,250	2,250	2,250	2,250
Other	2,000	167	167	167	167	167	167	167	167	167	167	167	167
TOTAL INCOME	376,735	27,708	30,708	32,708	32,708	32,708	32,708	32,708	32,708	32,708	29,787	29,787	29,787
EXPENSE													
Payroll Expense													
Salaries-Staff	270,000	22,759	23,793	20,690	23,793	23,793	20,690	21,724	22,759	22,759	21,724	23,793	21,724
Payroll Taxes	24,300	2,048	2,141	1,862	2,141	2,141	1,862	1,955	2,048	2,048	1,955	2,141	1,955
Worker's Comp	13,500	1,138	1,190	1,034	1,190	1,190	1,034	1,086	1,138	1,138	1,086	1,190	1,086
Staff Benefits													
Health Ins.	27,250	2,271	2,271	2,271	2,271	2,271	2,271	2,271	2,271	2,271	2,271	2,271	2,271
Dental Ins.	4,000	333	333	333	333	333	333	333	333	333	333	333	333
Education Allow.	875	73	73	73	73	73	73	73	73	73	73	73	73
Rent	4,800	400	400	400	400	400	400	400	400	400	400	400	400
Janitor	6,000	500	500	500	500	500	500	500	500	500	500	500	500
Insurance													
Liability	2,914	243	243	243	243	243	243	243	243	243	243	243	243
Accident	1,575	131	131	131	131	131	131	131	131	131	131	131	131
Directors Ins.	944	79	79	79	79	79	79	79	79	79	79	79	79
Supplies	15,000	1,250	1,250	1,250	1,250	1,250	1,250	1,250	1,250	1,250	1,250	1,250	1,250
Utilities	2,835	236	236	236	236	236	236	236	236	236	236	236	236
Capital Improvement	2,000	0	0	1,000	0	0	0	1,000	0	0	0	0	0
TOTAL EXPENSES	375,993	31,461	32,640	30,102	32,640	32,640	29,102	31,282	31,461	31,461	30,282	32,640	30,282
SURPLUS (DEFICIT)	742	(3,753)	(1,932)	2,606	68	68	3,606	1,427	1,247	1,247	(495)	(2,854)	(495)

Customize this form from the enclosed CD!

FIGURE 5–3 Felton Family Preschool Monthly Budget

January	23 paid days
February	20 paid days
March	21 paid days
April	22 paid days
May	22 paid days
June	21 paid days
July	23 paid days
August	21 paid days
Total paid days in the year	261 paid days

we can calculate the percentage of the total annual salary expense that we expect to spend in each month. Because there are 22 paid days in September, the salary expense for this month is estimated as 22 days divided by a total of 261 paid days in the year (22 divided by 261):

$$\frac{22 \text{ days}}{261 \text{ days}} = .084293$$

In other words, September's salary expense is expected to be 8.4293 percent of the total salaries for the year because September has 8.4293 percent of the total paid days.

Total annual salaries:	$270,000
September at 8.4293%:	$\times$ .084293
September's salary expense:	$22,759

In a similar way, we can calculate each month's percentage of the total budget and each month's salary expense for each of the other 11 months. This can be accomplished most easily in our spreadsheet itself, by building formulas in each of the 12 monthly cells (or boxes) of the salary line item. The formulas for each month are as follows:

month's salary expense = number of paid days in month divided by total paid days in year times annual salary budget,

or for the month of October:

23 paid days in Oct./261 paid days in year times $270,000, or
23/261 times the number in Cell D18 (23/261 $\times$ D18)

Notice that in our estimation of monthly salary expense we have not taken into account all of the ways in which this number will vary month to month. We have figured the difference month to month based on the *biggest* variance factor. It is possible to attempt to estimate other variables. However, to do so probably takes more time for a much smaller benefit than it is worth. At some point, you have to decide how far you will go to try to estimate a number down to the closest dollar, and when your estimate is *close enough* to serve your purpose. Just as it is true that for small programs a simple one-twelfth division of all expenses and income items is close enough, you have to decide how much time is worth spending to get an estimate that will work for you. And the more you do this, the better you will be at knowing how best to configure your budget.

Estimating Tuition Revenue

The estimate for tuition revenue also changes month to month as shown in Figure 5–4, and is based on your expectations and knowledge of past trends in enrollment. In our example,

			"Reasonable" Budget A3	September	October	November	December	January	February	March	April	May	June	July	August
Felton Family Preschool															
Monthly Budget															
INCOME															
Tuition			344,235	25,000	28,000	30,000	30,000	30,000	30,000	30,000	30,000	30,000	27,078	27,078	27,078
Fund-raising			3,500	292	292	292	292	292	292	292	292	292	292	292	292
County Grant			27,000	2,250	2,250	2,250	2,250	2,250	2,250	2,250	2,250	2,250	2,250	2,250	2,250
Other			2,000	167	167	167	167	167	167	167	167	167	167	167	167
TOTAL INCOME			376,735	27,708	30,708	32,708	32,708	32,708	32,708	32,708	32,708	32,708	29,787	29,787	29,787
EXPENSE															
Payroll Expense															
Salaries-Staff			270,000	22,759	23,793	20,690	23,793	23,793	20,690	21,724	22,759	22,759	21,724	23,793	21,724
Payroll Taxes			24,300	2,048	2,141	1,862	2,141	2,141	1,862	1,955	2,048	2,048	1,955	2,141	1,955
Worker's Comp			13,500	1,138	1,190	1,034	1,190	1,190	1,034	1,086	1,138	1,138	1,086	1,190	1,086
Staff Benefits															
Health Ins.			27,250	2,271	2,271	2,271	2,271	2,271	2,271	2,271	2,271	2,271	2,271	2,271	2,271
Dental Ins.			4,000	333	333	333	333	333	333	333	333	333	333	333	333
Education Allow.			875	73	73	73	73	73	73	73	73	73	73	73	73
Rent			4,800	400	400	400	400	400	400	400	400	400	400	400	400
Janitor			6,000	500	500	500	500	500	500	500	500	500	500	500	500
Insurance															
Liability			2,914	243	243	243	243	243	243	243	243	243	243	243	243
Accident			1,575	131	131	131	131	131	131	131	131	131	131	131	131
Directors Ins.			944	79	79	79	79	79	79	79	79	79	79	79	79
Supplies			15,000	1,250	1,250	1,250	1,250	1,250	1,250	1,250	1,250	1,250	1,250	1,250	1,250
Utilities			2,835	236	236	236	236	236	236	236	236	236	236	236	236
Capital Improvement			2,000	0	0	1,000	0	0	0	1,000	0	0	0	0	0
TOTAL EXPENSES			375,993	31,461	32,640	30,102	32,640	32,640	29,102	31,282	31,461	31,461	30,282	32,640	30,282
SURPLUS (DEFICIT)			742	(3,753)	(1,932)	2,606	68	68	3,606	1,427	1,247	1,247	(495)	(2,854)	(495)

Customize this form from the enclosed CD!

FIGURE 5–4 Felton Family Preschool Monthly Budget

✓ Hint

It is easier, and a close enough estimate, to use numbers that are rounded off to the nearest $100 or $1,000.

the first two months of the school year (September and October) and the summer months (June, July, August) have lower enrollment estimates than the other seven months. We know from past experience that during the first couple of months of each school year we are gradually enrolling families until we reach full enrollment around November. Enrollment usually declines in the summer months as our preschoolers leave the program. The tuition revenue amounts are rounded off to the nearest $1,000 in all but the last three months. Remember, we are making an *estimate* of these amounts. The tuition revenue amounts for June, July, and August were computed to balance the total of the twelve months to the annual budget total.

Because we are using unequal amounts in revenues and expenses in some months of the budget year, we are expecting deficits in the months of September, October, June, July, and August, while in the other months we project a surplus.

TRACKING REVENUE AND EXPENSE MONTH TO MONTH

Now that you have the annual budget divided into monthly amounts, whether on ledger paper, in a spreadsheet you have constructed separately, or incorporated within your accounting software (see the information box "Budget Tracking within Accounting Software," on page 81), you have a template for comparing what actually occurs month to month to what you have planned. *Do not* file your budget away in a drawer and leave it there unused for the year. It is *the* tool by which you track where your program stands financially. It tells you and your supervisor (board, corporation, clients, etc.) whether your enrollment is meeting expectations and is producing the level of income needed to pay for your planned expenses. It tells you whether expenses are within planned limits, and, if they are not, where you are spending too much. It is a document you should refer to frequently, at least monthly, to assess the financial position of your program. Post a hard copy of your monthly budget where you can see it. These numbers should be part of your everyday vocabulary.

Even the small home child care business can benefit from taking the time to track actual revenue and expense amounts against budget amounts every month. And, basically, the technique we will look at in the following sections is the same for *any* size business. In the next chapter we will explore simple ways for small businesses to record their monthly revenue and expense.

Figure 5–5 represents a portion of the monthly budget spreadsheet of Figure 5–1 in which columns have been inserted for each month's "Actual" and "Variance". This is done for all 12 months. You have already entered figures in the columns of the spreadsheet for the monthly budget numbers. These numbers do not change through the year. These numbers are the yardstick against which you want to measure what you are actually spending and actually receiving. At the end of each month, you will enter the actual totals for each of the revenue and expense items next to their budget amount. These actual figures will come from your accounting software or your ledgers in the form of a "profit and loss report" (in for-profit organizations) or an "income and expense statement" (in nonprofit organizations). These documents are discussed in full in the next chapter.

If you are able to enter budget numbers into your accounting software, the monthly financial reports produced from this software will automatically show the comparison between budget and actual numbers. In the spreadsheet in Figure 5–5, the "Variance" column is doing the same thing. It calculates the difference between what your budget said you should receive or spend and what actually happened. By reading this display carefully, you will know where you are drifting from your budget and by how much. It will help you to see when these differences are becoming so large as to negatively or positively affect your year-end financial results and your ability to continue the program as planned.

Felton Family Preschool
Two Months Budget Vs. Actual

	"Reasonable" Budget A3	September Budget	September Actual	September Variance	October Budget	October Actual	October Variance	2 Mos. Variance
INCOME								
Tuition	344,235	25,000	25,375	375	28,000	27,000	(1,000)	(625)
Fund-raising	3,500	292	50	(242)	292	0	(292)	(533)
County Grant	27,000	2,250	2,250	0	2,250	2,250	0	0
Other	2,000	167	200	33	167	100	(67)	(33)
TOTAL INCOME	376,735	27,708	27,875	167	30,708	29,350	(1,358)	(1,191)
EXPENSE								
Payroll Expense								
Salaries-Staff	270,000	22,759	24,410	(1,651)	23,793	25,130	(1,337)	(2,988)
Payroll Taxes	24,300	2,048	2,197	(149)	2,141	2,262	(120)	(269)
Worker's Comp	13,500	1,138	1,220	(83)	1,190	1,256	(67)	(149)
Staff Benefits								
Health Ins.	27,250	2,271	2,000	271	2,271	2,000	271	542
Dental Ins.	4,000	333	350	(17)	333	350	(17)	(33)
Education Allow.	875	73	0	73	73	100	(27)	46
Rent	4,800	400	400	0	400	400	0	0
Janitor	6,000	500	500	0	500	500	0	0
Insurance								
Liability	2,914	243	250	(7)	243	250	(7)	(14)
Accident	1,575	131	125	6	131	125	6	12
Directors Ins.	944	79	75	4	79	75	4	7
Supplies	15,000	1,250	640	610	1,250	2,000	(750)	(140)
Utilities	2,835	236	200	36	236	200	36	72
Capital Improvement	2,000	0	0	0	0	0	0	0
TOTAL EXPENSES	375,993	31,461	32,367	(906)	32,640	34,648	(2,008)	(2,914)
SURPLUS (DEFICIT)	742	(3,753)	(4,492)	(739)	(1,932)	(5,298)	(3,366)	(4,105)

FIGURE 5–5 Felton Family Preschool Two Months' Budgeted versus Actual

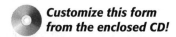

Customize this form from the enclosed CD!

Variances in Income and Expense

In all of the worksheets depicted in this book, "positive" variances are shown as numbers without a sign and "negative" variances are shown as numbers in parentheses. A variance in this context denotes the difference between two numbers. For income items, a positive variance means that the income amount actually earned was *greater* than the income amount that was budgeted. A negative variance in income means earnings were *less* than the budget.

For expense items, the variance works just the opposite: a positive variance in an expense item happens when spending is *less* than the budgeted amount. A negative variance in an expense means actual spending was *greater* than that budgeted.

The bottom line variance can be a bit trickier because it is possible the month's result will be a surplus, a positive number, or a deficit, a negative number. Just remember if the actual results are *better than* the budgeted results, the variance is positive. If the actual results are *not as good* as those in the budget, the variance is negative.

Tracking Actual Income and Expense: September

If you look at Column G, "September Variance," in the spreadsheet in Figure 5–5, you can see September tuition revenue was greater than budgeted tuition revenue for the month.

Actual September tuition revenue was	$25,375
Budgeted tuition revenue was expected to be	$25,000
The positive variance, or difference, is	$ 375

This variance tells you that you earned $375 more for the month in tuition revenue than you had budgeted. Your *total* revenue for the month of September was $167 greater than the budget.

Actual September total revenue was	$27,875
Budgeted total revenue was expected to be	$27,708
The positive variance, or difference, is	$ 167

Salaries for the month were $1,651 more than budget (Cell G16). Supplies were $610 less (Cell G29). Total expenses in September were $906 more than your budget.

Budgeted Expenses	$31,461
Actual Expenses	$32,367
Variance	($ 906)

Looking at the very bottom of the column labeled "September Actual," you see for the month of September your total deficit was $4,492. In the budget, you planned for a deficit of $3,753 for the month (bottom of column labeled "September Budget"). Your program's deficit was actually *greater* than budget by $739.

Actual September deficit was	($4,492)
Budgeted September deficit was	($3,753)
Negative variance is	($ 739)

This is a small negative variance. The Felton Preschool's budget for September seems to have been a good and accurate forecast. Costs were slightly over budget as a whole due exclusively to the fact that salaries were $1650 over budget for the month.

Budget Tracking within Accounting Software

Good computer accounting software will allow you to track actual revenues and expenses versus budgeted numbers. QuickBooks® (or QuickBooksPro®) software is an excellent tool for any small business and works very well in a child care organization. Budget figures are entered for each line item for each month. When preparing the monthly reports for income and expense you can select the "budget comparison reports" to print actual figures, budget figures, and the difference between the two in the same way as we have constructed the spreadsheet in Figure 5–5. (More about computer software in Chapter 6.)

! TIP

Note that even if your bottom line surplus or deficit is close to budget, this *does not necessarily mean* you do not have to look any further. There still could be expense items significantly over budget that are offset by other expenses under budget for the month. A quick review every month of the entire variance column is always a good idea.

Tracking Actual Income and Expense: October

After one month of operation into your new fiscal year, you feel expenses are within budget and enrollment and tuition revenue are at the expected levels. Let's move ahead one more month, and look at Figure 5–6 to see what has happened in October. The total for the month is as follows:

October deficit	($5,298)
Budgeted deficit for October	($1,932)
Negative variance	($3,366)

The loss in October was $3,366 *more than* you had budgeted. Right away, you should be alerted to look more closely to see what happened during the month to create this loss. You want to know whether it is merely a one-time, unexpected occurrence, or whether it may be the start of a trend that could jeopardize your program.

The loss in October of $5,298 is only 1.4 percent of your annual budget ($5,298 divided by $375,993). However, if October is the start of a trend that could continue for several more

Felton Family Preschool
Two Months Budget Vs. Actual

	"Reasonable" Budget A3	September Budget	September Actual	September Variance	October Budget	October Actual	October Variance	2 Mos. Variance
INCOME								
Tuition	344,235	25,000	25,375	375	28,000	27,000	(1,000)	(625)
Fund-raising	3,500	292	50	(242)	292	0	(292)	(533)
County Grant	27,000	2,250	2,250	0	2,250	2,250	0	0
Other	2,000	167	200	33	167	100	(67)	(33)
TOTAL INCOME	376,735	27,708	27,875	167	30,708	29,350	(1,358)	(1,191)
EXPENSE								
Payroll Expense								
Salaries-Staff	270,000	22,759	24,410	(1,651)	23,793	25,130	(1,337)	(2,988)
Payroll Taxes	24,300	2,048	2,197	(149)	2,141	2,262	(120)	(269)
Worker's Comp	13,500	1,138	1,220	(83)	1,190	1,256	(67)	(149)
Staff Benefits								
Health Ins.	27,250	2,271	2,000	271	2,271	2,000	271	542
Dental Ins.	4,000	333	350	(17)	333	350	(17)	(33)
Education Allow.	875	73	0	73	73	100	(27)	46
Rent	4,800	400	400	0	400	400	0	0
Janitor	6,000	500	500	0	500	500	0	0
Insurance								
Liability	2,914	243	250	(7)	243	250	(7)	(14)
Accident	1,575	131	125	6	131	125	6	12
Directors Ins.	944	79	75	4	79	75	4	7
Supplies	15,000	1,250	640	610	1,250	2,000	(750)	(140)
Utilities	2,835	236	200	36	236	200	36	72
Capital Improvement	2,000	0	0	0	0	0	0	0
TOTAL EXPENSES	375,993	31,461	32,367	(906)	32,640	34,648	(2,008)	(2,914)
SURPLUS (DEFICIT)	742	(3,753)	(4,492)	(739)	(1,932)	(5,298)	(3,366)	(4,105)

FIGURE 5–6 Felton Family Preschool Two Months' Budgeted versus Actual Financials

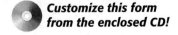
Customize this form from the enclosed CD!

months, this deficit will increase, and over three or four months' time would result in a much larger figure. If your program continued to lose $5,000 over the next four months, the total deficit for the months September through February would add up alarmingly, as we see below:

September deficit	$4,492
October deficit	$5,298
November–February deficits	$20,000
Total for six months	$29,790, or 8% of budget

By noticing the loss at this point, after only two months of operations, you are much better equipped to do something to stop the loss before too much time has passed. Not only is it easier to "fix" a deficit of approximately $10,000 than it is to fix a deficit of $30,000, but if you start working on a solution in November, you have nine more months to remedy the situation instead of only five more months if you waited until March.

Let's scan down the "October Variance" column (Column J) in Figure 5–6. October tuition revenue fell $1,000 short of your budget projection. Among all the categories of revenue, this variance is the most significant. A $292 variance in fund-raising revenue is not alarming, since the fund-raising events planned for the year have not yet occurred.

If we proceed down this variance column, the next number that is significant is the $1,337 negative variance in staff salaries. Again, by itself a one-month occurrence, it may not be important. But since this is the *second* month where there has been a negative variance in staff salaries (September staff salaries were $1,651 over budget), it may indicate a condition that over 6 to 12 months will have significant consequences for the entire budget. When tuition revenue is below budget we might suspect enrollment is below budget. If that is true, we also expect staff salaries to be *at or under* budget, not *greater* than budget.

For the two-month period, then, you have identified possible problems in two line items: tuition revenue and staff salaries. As was noted in the last chapter, these are always *the two most significant* line items in the budget of any child care program, and are the two line items that must be estimated most carefully. These are also the two items you must monitor most closely. A variance in either tuition revenue or staff salaries can determine the year's financial results. By noting both the tuition revenue and salaries have negative variances from our budget only two months into our fiscal year, you are in a good position to understand what may be going wrong and do something about it. If you had not been tracking your revenue and expenses monthly, and had only noticed the problem, say, six months into the year, the problem would be much more difficult to solve.

UNDERSTANDING VARIANCES AND PROBLEM SOLVING

The month-to-month comparison of actual revenue and expense to budgeted revenue and expense tells you *when* you have a variance, but not *why* you have a variance. For these kinds of answers you have to dig a little deeper and may need to review some of the supporting documents to your budget.

Operations at the End of Two Months

In Figure 5–7, the last column, labeled "2 Mos Variance," adds the monthly variances from September and October. As you scan down the column, you should again be looking for significantly large negative numbers (i.e., numbers in parentheses). In the revenue section, a negative variance indicates what has been received is *less than* what had been budgeted as

	"Reasonable" Budget A3	September Budget	September Actual	September Variance	October Budget	October Actual	October Variance	2 Mos. Variance
Felton Family Preschool								
Budget Vs. Actual								
INCOME								
Tuition	344,235	25,000	25,375	375	28,000	27,000	(1,000)	(625)
Fund-raising	3,500	292	50	(242)	292	0	(292)	(533)
County Grant	27,000	2,250	2,250	0	2,250	2,250	0	0
Other	2,000	167	200	33	167	100	(67)	(33)
TOTAL INCOME	376,735	27,708	27,875	167	30,708	29,350	(1,358)	(1,191)
EXPENSE								
Payroll Expense								
Salaries-Staff	270,000	22,759	24,410	(1,651)	23,793	25,130	(1,337)	(2,988)
Payroll Taxes	24,300	2,048	2,197	(149)	2,141	2,262	(120)	(269)
Worker's Comp	13,500	1,138	1,220	(83)	1,190	1,256	(67)	(149)
Staff Benefits								
Health Ins.	27,250	2,271	2,000	271	2,271	2,000	271	542
Dental Ins.	4,000	333	350	(17)	333	350	(17)	(33)
Education Allow.	875	73	0	73	73	100	(27)	46
Rent	4,800	400	400	0	400	400	0	0
Janitor	6,000	500	500	0	500	500	0	0
Insurance								
Liability	2,914	243	250	(7)	243	250	(7)	(14)
Accident	1,575	131	125	6	131	125	6	12
Directors Ins.	944	79	75	4	79	75	4	7
Supplies	15,000	1,250	640	610	1,250	2,000	(750)	(140)
Utilities	2,835	236	200	36	236	200	36	72
Capital Improvement	2,000	0	0	0	0	0	0	0
TOTAL EXPENSES	375,993	31,461	32,367	(906)	32,640	34,648	(2,008)	(2,914)
SURPLUS (DEFICIT)	742	(3,753)	(4,492)	(739)	(1,932)	(5,298)	(3,366)	(4,105)

FIGURE 5–7 Felton Family Preschool Budget versus Actual

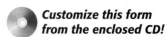

Customize this form from the enclosed CD!

revenue. In the expense section, a negative variance indicates spending in that category has been *greater than* you had budgeted.

The total income for the months of September and October is $1,191 below the budget plan (Column K, line labeled "Total Income"). This variance for total income is negative primarily because both tuition revenue and fund-raising revenue are below budget. You may not need to worry at this point about the fund-raising revenue. Fund-raising income is earned in those months during or immediately following the fund-raising event. If the event has not yet occurred, there will not yet be any income recorded. Tuition revenue, however, although slightly above budget in September, did not increase in October as much as had been planned.

October budgeted tuition income	$28,000
October actual tuition income	$27,000

By going to the revenue estimating spreadsheet (Figure 4–7) and your current enrollment statistics, you should be able to see in which age group or in which program you are underenrolled. It could be a temporary setback—for example, a child was delayed in enrolling until November, or a child unexpectedly exited the program, or two children changed from full-time to part-time schedules. Whatever has happened, you cannot know what it is or how to fix it from looking at your budget. But you can find out whether there is a problem and in what category there is a problem. By using the supporting spreadsheets constructed during the budgeting process, you can determine exactly what has happened and where enrollment is not meeting your plan.

A negative variance in tuition revenue is the usual cause of business distress in home child care. If you are able to keep enough children in your program and to charge enough for their care, a home child care owner can earn enough to cover all costs including a reasonable salary. This is the line item that should be monitored *every* month even if little attention is paid to all other items.

In our example, the variance in staff salaries for the two months is ($2,988). This negative variance is 1.1 percent of the annual salary budget. In September and in October your program spent more on salaries than you had budgeted. Is this a trend starting? Why are you spending more on salaries, when your enrollment is below what you had anticipated for October? Is it in overtime for staff meetings? Is it substitute salaries? These are questions that, again, cannot be answered by looking at your budget and the variances. You must go to your supporting documents—the staff salary spreadsheet (Figure 4–4) and your payroll records—to see where you are spending over budget so you can do something about it.

Operations After Seven Months

In Figure 5–8 we have jumped ahead in time to see the results of budget versus actual numbers seven months into the fiscal year. Column D restates our annual budget. The second column of figures is our budget for seven months, that is, what we expect to receive and spend after seven months of operation, September through March. Column G, "Sept–March Actual," tells us what we have actually received and spent in each of the line item categories. Column H gives us the variance, or difference, between what had been budgeted and what actually happened.

By scanning down the variance column again, notice both tuition income and fund-raising income have positive variances. We have received $5,122 in fund-raising income already, which is greater than the total amount forecast for the year. Our tuition revenue is $2,525 greater than budget for the seven months. Our total income for the seven months is thus $5,430 greater than we had planned for the seven months through the end of March. As long as we can continue to keep enrollment at current levels, we can expect to end the year ahead of our plan in total income.

On the expense side, staff salaries are now slightly under budget. For the seven months of operation through March, we have spent $921 less than budget. As enrollment has been higher than our projections, we are doing well to have slightly lower staffing costs.

Expenses for supplies and utilities have been running over budget. Utility costs may be higher because we have just been through the winter months and have had higher heating costs than we will in the remaining five months of the year. This variance is probably worth exploring further to determine why it is negative. It may or may not be a problem needing attention. We should also monitor our supplies spending over the next few months if we are going to keep the total spending in this category within our budgeted amount for the year. Remember, however, that a negative variance in these categories is not really significant in the bigger picture since the dollar value here is relatively small. For most busy administrators, it is advisable to focus on the large budget items and not waste time solving the smaller budget issues.

The most significant cost saving so far this year in expenses other than staffing costs, is in capital improvements, where there is a positive variance of $800 at the end of March. It may have been our intention to control spending in this category until we could see how actual revenue and expense compared to budget through the year. Or it may be that our planned spending for capital improvements has been delayed for other reasons.

Felton Family Preschool
Example 1: Results After 7 Months

	"Reasonable" Budget A3	Sept–March Budget	Sept–March Actual	Sept–March Variance
INCOME				
Tuition	344,235	203,000	205,525	2,525
Fund-raising	3,500	2,042	5,122	3,080
County Grant	27,000	15,750	15,750	0
Other	2,000	1,167	992	(175)
TOTAL INCOME	376,735	221,959	227,389	5,430
EXPENSE				
Payroll Expense				
Salaries-Staff	270,000	157,241	156,320	921
Payroll Taxes	24,300	14,152	13,287	865
Worker's Comp	13,500	7,862	7,816	46
Staff Benefits				
Health Ins.	27,250	15,896	15,721	175
Dental Ins.	4,000	2,333	2,350	(17)
Education Allow.	875	510	585	(75)
Rent	4,800	2,800	2,800	0
Janitor	6,000	3,500	3,500	0
Insurance				
Liability	2,914	1,700	1,700	(0)
Accident	1,575	919	925	(6)
Directors Ins.	944	551	550	1
Supplies	15,000	8,750	11,322	(2,572)
Utilities	2,835	1,654	2,240	(586)
Capital Improvement	2,000	2,000	1,200	800
TOTAL EXPENSES	375,993	219,868	220,316	(448)
SURPLUS (DEFICIT)	742	2,091	7,073	4,982

FIGURE 5–8 Felton Family Preschool Example 1: Results After Seven Months of Operations

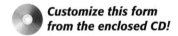

Customize this form from the enclosed CD!

If our results for seven months of operations are those that appear in Figure 5–8, we may now want to make some changes to operations. We may, for example, decide to go ahead with the budgeted capital improvement spending. We may decide to plan a professional development day for staff where paid speakers are brought in to the center to present workshops. We may plan to purchase additional curriculum material. Or, we may decide to continue operating as we have been since September in the anticipation of ending the year with a larger surplus than we had intended when we constructed the budget. This surplus will be added to our cash reserves (see information box) at the end of the year as a safety net for any unanticipated drop in income or increase in expenses.

Operations After Seven Months, Example Two

Let's now assume that operations have not been as smooth as depicted in Figure 5–8. The next worksheet, Figure 5–9, shows a different picture of what the revenues and expenses have been over the first seven months of the fiscal year. At the bottom of column F, "Sept–March Actual," we see the center has a deficit of $8,768 at the end of March. Because we had budgeted to have a small surplus of $2,091 by this time, our variance to budget is a negative $10,859 (a *minus* $8,768 minus $2,091).

Cash Reserves

■ Cash savings held in an interest-bearing account.

■ Usually set to equal one to three months' operating expenses. (In our example, expenses are approximately $30,000 per month. A three-month reserve would thus equal $90,000.)

■ Used only in emergencies or to cover temporary cash-flow shortages.

Felton Family Preschool
Example 2: Results After 7 Months' Operation

	"Reasonable" Budget A3	Sept–March Budget	Sept–March Actual	Sept–March Variance
INCOME				
Tuition	344,235	203,000	192,500	(10,500)
Fund-raising	3,500	2,042	1,000	(1,042)
County Grant	27,000	15,750	15,750	0
Other	2,000	1,167	992	(175)
TOTAL INCOME	376,735	221,959	210,242	(11,717)
EXPENSE				
Payroll Expense				
Salaries-Staff	270,000	157,241	158,033	(792)
Payroll Taxes	24,300	14,152	13,433	719
Worker's Comp	13,500	7,862	7,902	(40)
Staff Benefits				
Health Ins.	27,250	15,896	17,252	(1,356)
Dental Ins.	4,000	2,333	2,350	(17)
Education Allow.	875	510	585	(75)
Rent	4,800	2,800	2,800	0
Janitor	6,000	3,500	3,500	0
Insurance				
Liability	2,914	1,700	1,700	0
Accident	1,575	919	925	(6)
Directors Ins.	944	551	550	1
Supplies	15,000	8,750	6,540	2,210
Utilities	2,835	1,654	2,240	(586)
Capital Improvement	2,000	2,000	1,200	800
TOTAL EXPENSES	375,993	219,868	219,010	858
SURPLUS (DEFICIT)	742	2,091	(8,768)	(10,859)

FIGURE 5–9 Felton Family Preschool Example 2: Results After Seven Months of Operation

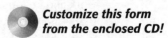

Customize this form from the enclosed CD!

What does this actually mean and why should we be concerned about a loss of nearly $9,000? At some point, we will have to take money out of our reserves, assuming we have cash reserves, to fund this year's operations. If we are earning less money than we are spending, we are not able to fund current operations out of current revenue. We will have to bring in additional cash to pay for our expenses. Any small business should try to maintain from one month's to three months' operating expenses in a reserve to help out in emergency situations. Depending on how much money we actually have in reserve, at some point these funds will be depleted. Or, possibly, there is no reserve to begin with. Eventually we will run out of money, we will run out of cash, and will no longer have enough money to fund payroll or to keep our program open.

What do we do at this point? There are still five more months in the year. We may not be able to erase completely the deficit we have accumulated so far, but we can probably diminish it. But, remember, we are already expecting to run deficits in June, July, and August. If that happens, we have a greater need to either

increase income, or

decrease spending.

And we have to do it quickly, as every day, every week we delay our decision, we may be losing more money. If we had been monitoring our financial results on a monthly basis, we would not have allowed our deficit to grow this large; we would have already made some changes to operations. By using such an extreme example, however, we will be able to explore how to go about ending the losses and even "making up" the deficit to reduce it by year-end. This process will illustrate the kinds of drastic measures necessitated by allowing a problem to continue so long and not facing it head-on earlier in the year. Hopefully, you will never let your program get in this position.

The same method is used in this situation to determine where we have a problem. Scanning down the last column in Figure 5–9, "Sept–March Variance," we find our largest problem immediately. Our tuition revenue to date is $10,500 behind where it should be. Remember, this is *the* most crucial component of income. We cannot expect to finance our program if our enrollment is well below capacity. Or, at least, we cannot expect to run our program in the manner we are used to, if we are not using our enrollment capacity.

A negative variance of $10,500 in our tuition revenue over seven months means that *on average* monthly revenue was less than our monthly budget by $1,500 (10,500 divided by 7 months). This is not a large amount. It represents only about two full-time children. If our enrollment has been consistently below the budgeted enrollment by only about two children since we started the fiscal year, it is easy to see how we could have overlooked this shortfall. But in an organization this size you can see the significance of the impact even a small shortfall in enrollment can have over a period of several months. In smaller centers, the impact of one or two less children can have an even greater impact on the bottom line. It is also possible that our enrollment has only dropped in the last couple of months by about $5,000 each month. Now it is the end of March and because we failed to notice our enrollment was not meeting the planned levels we have a large deficit and a short time frame in which to fix it.

There can be any number of other reasons why our tuition revenue is well below budget. We may be experiencing the effects of a slow economy, where parents are out of work and no longer need or can afford full-time child care. It is possible our mix of students, that is, how many children are enrolled in each age group in each schedule, is very different from what we had forecast in our budget planning. Perhaps we have enrolled too many "reduced-rate" children and have fewer families paying the full rates for care. We must examine the details of our current enrollment to determine the exact causes of our deficit and find some ways of addressing the problem to increase enrollment numbers.

"Fixing" enrollment can certainly take longer than a couple of weeks. It may not be possible to realize any benefits from enrolling more children for at least a month, and, depending on circumstances, we may not be able to increase enrollment substantially this fiscal year at all. Tuition rate increases are rarely considered midyear, especially when we have already failed to fill our center at current rates. So, what do we do?

We notice, too, that the fund-raising income is not meeting budget. We can increase efforts to raise more funds by the end of the year. But this effort may only increase our income by $2,000 to $4,000 even if we are unusually successful. We must look to the cost side of our budget to find ways in which we can cut spending, at least temporarily, so we are operating month to month at a surplus. This is the only way to stop the year's deficit from growing larger. Our goal at this point is actually to *decrease* the size of our loss by the end of August.

Turning a Large Deficit into a Not-so-large Deficit

Moving further down the variance column (Column G) in Figure 5–10, we see only small negative variances on the expense side. Staff salaries are $792 over budget after seven months and health insurance expense is $1,356 over budget. Since the salary variance is only .5 percent of our year-to-date salary budget ($792 divided by $154,135), by itself this

	A	B	C	D	E	F	G	H
1								
2		Felton Family Preschool						
3		Example 2: Results After 7 Months' Operation						
4								
5				"Reasonable"	Sept–March	Sept–March	Sept–March	
6				Budget A3	Budget	Actual	Variance	
7								
8		INCOME						
9		Tuition		344,235	203,000	192,500	(10,500)	
10		Fund-raising		3,500	2,042	1,000	(1,042)	
11		County Grant		27,000	15,750	15,750	0	
12		Other		2,000	1,167	992	(175)	
13								
14		TOTAL INCOME		376,735	221,959	210,242	(11,717)	
15								
16		EXPENSE						
17		Payroll Expense						
18		Salaries-Staff		270,000	157,241	158,033	(792)	
19		Payroll Taxes		24,300	14,152	13,433	719	
20		Worker's Comp		13,500	7,862	7,902	(40)	
21		Staff Benefits						
22		Health Ins.		27,250	15,896	17,252	(1,356)	
23		Dental Ins.		4,000	2,333	2,350	(17)	
24		Education Allow.		875	510	585	(75)	
25		Rent		4,800	2,800	2,800	0	
26		Janitor		6,000	3,500	3,500	0	
27		Insurance						
28		Liability		2,914	1,700	1,700	0	
29		Accident		1,575	919	925	(6)	
30		Directors Ins.		944	551	550	1	
31		Supplies		15,000	8,750	6,540	2,210	
32		Utilities		2,835	1,654	2,240	(586)	
33								
34		Capital Improvement		2,000	2,000	1,200	800	
35		**TOTAL EXPENSES**		375,993	219,868	219,010	858	
36								
37		**SURPLUS (DEFICIT)**		742	2,091	(8,768)	(10,859)	
38								

FIGURE 5–10 Felton Family Preschool Example 2: Results After Seven Months of Operation

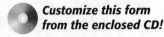

Customize this form from the enclosed CD!

is not a noteworthy amount. However, because we are running *under* budget in tuition revenue, thus by inference we are not fully enrolled, we expect our staffing needs should not be greater than we planned.

As was discussed in the last chapter, spending in staff salaries and benefits is the most important factor in our total expense budget. Because most of our dollars are used here, this is where we can potentially save the most money. As difficult a decision as it is for child care administrators, we must find ways to trim staff costs when necessary; in this example we must do so if we hope to diminish the size of the year-to-date deficit by the end of August. Once enrollment is increased, we will be able to add back to staff what we have had to take away.

In order to *eliminate* the $8,768 deficit in our example, the program must earn a surplus in each of the next five months of approximately $1,754 ($8,768 deficit divided by 5 remaining months of our year equals $1,754). We can add on to our spreadsheet in Figure 5–10

The Children's Center: A Case Study

A small child care center in Santa Cruz County faced a serious situation in the fall of 2002. Tuition revenue and county funding were not producing sufficient income to cover the costs of operation at this center serving approximately 60 families. In each of the first three months of their fiscal year, the center ran a deficit. With only a small cash reserve, the center was just able to cover payroll and other necessary expenses every month.

Under such difficult conditions, their community rallied together. Initially, the board of directors voted to implement a 10 percent pay cut for all staff. The board decided this was the only way to achieve an immediate impact on the accumulated deficit. They could see no other way to trim spending so the effect would be large enough to make an immediate difference. Staff of the center, however, did not want the pay cut and brought their concerns to an emergency board meeting. In response, the board established a task force comprised of staff, and including the director and board members, to determine if there were any other ways to cut spending without having to cut staff salaries. If the task force could find monthly savings that equalled or exceeded the amount to be gained by the proposed pay cut, the board would take this alternate plan under consideration.

The task force was successful in its efforts. Guided by the director, the members of the task force looked at staffing, staff schedules, ratios, breaks, naptimes, and overlaps between morning teachers and afternoon teachers. As a group, they agreed on several small measures that together amounted to slightly more sav-

ings per month than a pay cut would realize. These measures are listed below:

1) Eliminate the afternoon part-time food worker (director would prepare afternoon snack and do kitchen cleanup);

2) Reduce staff overlap of morning and afternoon shifts from one hour to fifteen minutes;

3) Move from 1/6 ratio in the 3–5-year-old room, to 1/8 ratio, which would reduce the number of teacher hours in that classroom;

4) Reduce size of "nap window," i.e., time during which children are napping, in toddler room by one hour, again a saving in staff hours;

5) Institute the "red-dot" system: when the number of children attending declined due to illness or children going home early, a rotating red dot would designate which staff member would leave early or come in late that day. In other words, staffing only for children *attending*, not for full enrollment;

6) Temporarily eliminate paid staff meeting time.

None of these changes by themselves could realize enough of a savings to eliminate the monthly deficits, but all of them taken together did so. The board voted to accept this alternate plan, and no pay cuts were instituted. If enrollment and income increased at some point, the director could reevaluate the above cost-saving measures.

with columns for the months of April through August. In these columns we will plan our targets for each of the months in the future and determine exactly how much savings we can make each month. This has been done in Figure 5–11.

Column H, "Average per Month," tells us for each line item of revenue and expense what the average was over the past seven months. Column H contains a formula that divides the numbers in Column F, "Sept–March Actual," by seven. If we assume that every line item in revenue and expense *except staff salaries, fundraising income, and capital improvement expense* will equal this average figure in each of the next five months of the year, we can determine what staff salaries must equal in order to arrive at a net surplus each month of approximately $1,750. For fund-raising income, we will assume that a planned event in early June will raise $1,000; no other fund-raising income is expected for the year. We will also assume that no further expenditures are made for capital improvements.

In order to reach an approximate $1,750 surplus target each month, salaries for staff must be reduced to $19,800 per month. We have "backed into" this number, estimating what all other line items will be first and knowing the monthly surplus that is our goal. In the budget spreadsheet in Figure 5–7, I used trial and error, guessing the salary cost to see the effect on the bottom line. I started with a very low number, $18,000. When I entered $18,000 as the salary expense figure in Cells I19 through M19 the spreadsheet calculated a net surplus for the end of the year of $8,993. Since I am trying to reach a year-end deficit of $0, this calculation told me that the $18,000 figure was too low. Then I tried $19,000 as the salary expense number, and continued to try different figures in those cells until I reached the numbers shown in Figure 5–11. If salary expense can be reduced to this level, we would end the year at approximately break-even.

Salary expense of $19,800 each month represents a reduction of approximately $2,800 from the average we have spent each month through March.

Average salary expense per month was	$22,576
Proposed monthly salary expense	$19,800
Difference is	$ 2,776

Is a reduction of $2,800 per month, or about 12 percent of our monthly salary budget ($2,800 divided by $22,576), a feasible reduction? About how many staff hours does this

Average Hourly Wage Rate

In Figure 5–12, the average hourly wage rate is computed for the Felton Family Preschool. This is a statistic that can help you simplify many estimates you may want to make in determining staffing costs. It can be used to figure quickly the cost of staff, and savings in staff costs, rather than having to calculate different costs for different staff at different rates of pay. The computation can be accomplished very simply by hand or in a spreadsheet using a method called "weighted average."

Begin with the staffing spreadsheet (Figure 4–4 from the previous chapter) that was constructed to estimate staff costs for our budget. Figure 5–12 is this same spreadsheet with Column H added. In Column H each employee's current rate of pay is multiplied by the number of hours they work each week. This is the "weighted" part of the average computation. The formulas thus give more "weight" to those rates of pay for which particular employees work more hours. By totaling all the numbers in Column H and dividing this total by the total hours worked by all staff in a week (460 hours), the average rate of pay for all staff at the center is calculated to be $10.72.

Felton Family Preschool

Example 2: Forecasting the Remaining Five Months

	"Reasonable" Budget A3	Sept–March Budget	Sept–March Actual	Sept–March Variance	Average per Month	April Plan	May Plan	June Plan	July Plan	August Plan	Year-end Total
INCOME											
Tuition	344,235	203,000	192,500	(10,500)	27,500	27,500	27,500	27,500	27,500	27,500	330,000
Fund-raising	3,500	2,042	1,000	(1,042)	143	0	0	1,000	0	0	2,000
County Grant	27,000	15,750	15,750	0	2,250	2,250	2,250	2,250	2,250	2,250	27,000
Other	2,000	1,167	992	(175)	142	142	142	142	142	142	1,701
TOTAL INCOME	376,735	221,959	210,242	(11,717)	30,035	29,892	29,892	30,892	29,892	29,892	360,701
EXPENSE											
Payroll Expense											
Salaries-Staff	270,000	157,241	158,033	(792)	22,576	19,800	19,800	19,800	19,800	19,800	257,033
Payroll Taxes	24,300	14,152	13,433	719	1,919	1,919	1,919	1,919	1,919	1,919	23,028
Worker's Comp	13,500	7,862	7,902	(40)	1,129	1,129	1,129	1,129	1,129	1,129	13,546
Staff Benefits											
Health Ins.	27,250	15,896	17,252	(1,356)	2,465	2,465	2,465	2,465	2,465	2,465	29,575
Dental Ins.	4,000	2,333	2,350	(17)	336	336	336	336	336	336	4,029
Education Allow.	875	510	585	(75)	84	84	84	84	84	84	1,003
Rent	4,800	2,800	2,800	0	400	400	400	400	400	400	4,800
Janitor	6,000	3,500	3,500	0	500	500	500	500	500	500	6,000
Insurance											
Liability	2,914	1,700	1,700	0	243	243	243	243	243	243	2,914
Accident	1,575	919	925	(6)	132	132	132	132	132	132	1,586
Directors Ins.	944	551	550	1	79	79	79	79	79	79	943
Supplies	15,000	8,750	6,540	2,210	934	934	934	934	934	934	11,211
Utilities	2,835	1,654	2,240	(586)	320	320	320	320	320	320	3,840
Capital Improvement	2,000	2,000	1,200	800	171	0	0	0	0	0	1,200
TOTAL EXPENSES	375,993	219,867	219,010	857	31,287	28,340	28,340	28,340	28,340	28,340	360,708
SURPLUS (DEFICIT)	742	2,092	(8,768)	(10,860)	(1,253)	1,552	1,552	2,552	1,552	1,552	(7)

Customize this form from the enclosed CD!

FIGURE 5–11 Example 2: Forecasting the Remaining Five Months of the Year

Felton Family Preschool
Average Wage Rate

Employee	Current Wage Rate	Budget Wage Rate	Hours/Wk	Annual Salary		Average Hourly Wage
Latifa	$11.00	$12.00	40	$24,960		$480.00
Sheena	$9.50	$10.00	30	$15,600		$300.00
Carol	$8.00	$9.00	40	$18,720		$360.00
Jean-Claude	$10.50	$11.00	35	$20,020		$385.00
Marta	$10.00	$10.50	20	$10,920		$210.00
				$90,220	Total Toddler Staff	
Francis	$9.00	$10.00	40	$20,800		$400.00
Georgia	$9.00	$9.50	30	$14,820		$285.00
Janisha	$11.00	$11.50	30	$17,940		$345.00
Juan	$11.00	$12.00	40	$24,960		$480.00
				$78,520	Total Young Preschool	
Director/Teacher	$12.00	$13.00	10	$6,760		$130.00
Isabel	$10.00	$11.00	40	$22,880		$440.00
Jodie	$9.75	$10.50	35	$19,110		$367.50
Linda	$8.00	$9.00	40	$18,720		$360.00
				$67,470	Total Pre-K Staff	
Director/Teacher	$12.00	$13.00	30	$20,280		$390.00
Substitutes				$13,510		
			460	$270,000	TOTAL SALARIES	$10.72

FIGURE 5–12 Computation of Felton Family Preschool Average Wage Rate

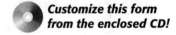

Customize this form from the enclosed CD!

represent each month? If we assume an average hourly wage rate (see information box) paid to staff of $10.72, a reduction of $2,800 represents a reduction of about 261 staff hours per month ($2,800 divided by $10.72 = 261 hours).

A reduction of 261 hours per month is a considerable reduction in staff hours for our center and is probably not a reasonable target if we are hoping to retain the quality of care we are now providing. If we know that all staff work a total of 460 hours *per week* (see Figure 5–12, bottom of Column E), 261 hours *per month* represents more than one-half of a full week out of every month we would be cutting. Rather than cutting staff hours so drastically, we may want to test a reduction of a fewer number of staff hours, say 125 staff hours per month. A reduction of 125 staff hours, at our average wage rate of $10.72 per hour,

$$(125 \text{ hours} \times \$10.72 \text{ per hour}),$$

is a savings of $1,340 per month. Staff salaries on average would then equal

$$\$22,576 \text{ minus } \$1,340, \text{ or } \$21,236 \text{ per month}.$$

Figure 5–13 takes the same year-to-date figures we had in Figure 5–9 and incorporates this new salary figure in the months of April through August in the salaries line. Unfortunately, by reducing the monthly salary expense by $1,340, we would still end the year with a deficit of $6,282.

Felton Family Preschool

Reducing the Operating Deficit

	"Reasonable" Budget A3	Sept–March Budget	Sept–March Actual	Sept–March Variance	Average per Month	April Plan	May Plan	June Plan	July Plan	August Plan	Year-end Total
INCOME											
Tuition	344,235	203,000	192,500	(10,500)	27,500	27,500	27,500	27,500	27,500	27,500	330,000
Fund-raising	3,500	2,042	1,000	(1,042)	143	0	0	1,000	0	0	2,000
County Grant	27,000	15,750	15,750	0	2,250	2,250	2,250	2,250	2,250	2,250	27,000
Other	2,000	1,167	992	(175)	142	142	142	142	142	142	1,701
TOTAL INCOME	376,735	221,959	210,242	(11,717)	30,035	29,892	29,892	30,892	29,892	29,892	360,701
EXPENSE											
Payroll Expense											
Salaries-Staff	270,000	157,241	158,033	(792)	22,576	21,236	21,236	21,236	21,236	21,236	264,213
Payroll Taxes	24,300	14,152	13,433	719	1,919	1,805	1,805	1,805	1,805	1,805	22,458
Worker's Comp	13,500	7,862	7,902	(40)	1,129	1,062	1,062	1,062	1,062	1,062	13,211
Staff Benefits											
Health Ins.	27,250	15,896	17,252	(1,356)	2,465	2,465	2,465	2,465	2,465	2,465	29,575
Dental Ins.	4,000	2,333	2,350	(17)	336	336	336	336	336	336	4,029
Education Allow.	875	510	585	(75)	84	84	84	84	84	84	1,003
Rent	4,800	2,800	2,800	0	400	400	400	400	400	400	4,800
Janitor	6,000	3,500	3,500	0	500	500	500	500	500	500	6,000
Insurance											
Liability	2,914	1,700	1,700	0	243	243	243	243	243	243	2,914
Accident	1,575	919	925	(6)	132	132	132	132	132	132	1,586
Directors Ins.	944	551	550	1	79	79	79	79	79	79	943
Supplies	15,000	8,750	6,540	2,210	934	934	934	934	934	934	11,211
Utilities	2,835	1,654	2,240	(586)	320	320	320	320	320	320	3,840
Capital Improvement	2,000	2,000	1,200	800	171	0	0	0	0	0	1,200
TOTAL EXPENSES	375,993	219,868	219,010	858	31,287	29,595	29,595	29,595	29,595	29,595	366,983
SURPLUS (DEFICIT)	742	2,091	(8,768)	(10,859)	(1,252)	297	297	1,297	297	297	(6,282)

FIGURE 5–13 Example 2: Planning How to Reduce Operating Deficit

Customize this form from the enclosed CD!

Notice in Figure 5–13 the numbers have also changed in Rows 20 and 21 where payroll tax and worker's compensation insurance is listed. That is because I have added a formula in the cells on these rows for Columns I through M to calculate both these figures based on a percentage of the salary figure as we did when first constructing our budget. Since salaries are lower, both payroll taxes and worker's compensation will be lower. Payroll tax is computed at 8.5 percent of the salary line, as that is what it has been running all year to this point. Worker's compensation insurance is calculated as $5.00 per $100 of salary, or

salary *divided by* 100 *times* $5.

The expense for these categories has come down as the amount spent on salaries is reduced.

Now, considering we are still looking at a deficit at year-end, several questions must be addressed, and, *depending on one's particular situation*, the answers could be quite different from program to program.

Question 1: Is a year-end deficit of $6,282 acceptable?   If our cash reserves are sufficient to cover such a deficit, our answer might be yes. This is the kind of situation for which our reserves are planned. We might want to look at the larger economic picture and assess our program's ability to attract students and maintain enrollment. Would we rather tighten our belts now by cutting costs to a greater degree so our year-end loss will be smaller even though we could cover a $6,282 deficit with reserves?

Question 2: Is a reduction of 125 staff hours a month something that can be accomplished without jeopardizing program quality?   By breaking down this number on a daily basis, we can get a feel for what this really means. If an average month has 22 workdays, 125 hours per month would be approximately 5.68 hours per day (125 hours divided by 22 days), or the equivalent of a little less than a full-time teacher who is earning the *average* wage rate. If a staff member earns more than the average rate, then their time could be cut by fewer hours to gain the same cost savings.

Example:

Staff member earning $10.72 × 6 hours = $64.32 savings

Staff member earning $12.00 × 5.36 hours = $64.32 savings

If we think this reduction in staff hours is reasonable considering our current enrollment, then we could proceed to determine exactly where reductions can be made.

In our example, if the staff and salaries are as shown in Figure 5–14, we may decide to make the following changes in order to realize the necessary savings:

Linda: reduce hours to 35 per week, save 1 hour/day	= $ 9.00
Jodie: reduce hours to 30 per week, save 1 hour/day	= $10.50
Director: add in 1 hour/day, no effect on costs	
Francis: reduce hours to 35 per week, save 1 hour/day	= $10.00
Juan: reduce hours to 35 per week, save 1 hour/day	= $12.00

Additional cuts needed, as shown below:

Latifa: reduce hours to 37.5/wk, save 1/2 hour/day	= $6.00
Marta: reduce hours to 17.5/wk, save 1/2 hour/day	= $5.25
Jean-Claude: reduce hours to 32.5/wk, save 1/2 hour/day	= $5.50

Total savings net salaries	=	$58.25 day
# days/month	×	22
Total salary savings/month	=	$1,282

Felton Family Preschool
Staff Salaries

	Employee	Current Wage Rate	Budget Wage Rate	Hours/Wk	Annual Salary		Average Hourly Wage
8	Latifa	$11.00	$12.00	40	$24,960		$480.00
9	Sheena	$9.50	$10.00	30	$15,600		$300.00
10	Carol	$8.00	$9.00	40	$18,720		$360.00
11	Jean-Claude	$10.50	$11.00	35	$20,020		$385.00
12	Marta	$10.00	$10.50	20	$10,920		$210.00
13							
14					$90,220	Total Toddler Staff	
15							
16	Francis	$9.00	$10.00	40	$20,800		$400.00
17	Georgia	$9.00	$9.50	30	$14,820		$285.00
18	Janisha	$11.00	$11.50	30	$17,940		$345.00
19	Juan	$11.00	$12.00	40	$24,960		$480.00
20							
21					$78,520	Total Young Preschool	
22							
23	Director/Teacher	$12.00	$13.00	10	$6,760		$130.00
24	Isabel	$10.00	$11.00	40	$22,880		$440.00
25	Jodie	$9.75	$10.50	35	$19,110		$367.50
26	Linda	$8.00	$9.00	40	$18,720		$360.00
27							
28					$67,470	Total Pre-K Staff	
29							
30	Director/Teacher	$12.00	$13.00	30	$20,280		$390.00
31	Substitutes				$13,510		
32							
33				460	$270,000	TOTAL SALARIES	$10.72
34							

FIGURE 5–14 Felton Family Preschool Staff Salaries

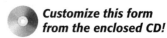

Customize this form from the enclosed CD!

Salary expense per month would then be

$22,576 minus $1,282, or $21,294.

Question 3: Are there additional savings that can be realized? By looking at other cost categories in Figure 5–15, we may be able to find additional cost savings. For example, if we believe by year-end we will not exceed our budgeted amount for utilities because traditionally the spring and summer months have cost us less, then we can reestimate the cost of utilities over the next five months. Instead of running at the winter's average rate, we can estimate that the cost of utilities each month from April through August would equal one-fifth of the difference between what we have spent year-to-date, and what our total annual budget is for this line item.

Year's budget for utilities	=	$2,835
minus Year-to-date utility expense	=	$2,240
Remaining utility cost	=	$ 595
Divided by 5 more months equals cost per month	=	119

It may also be possible to curb spending in supplies for the remainder of the year by close monitoring of classroom budgets. Rather than spending the average of $934

Felton Family Preschool

Example 2: Further Cost Savings

	"Reasonable" Budget A3	Sept–March Budget	Sept–March Actual	Sept–March Variance	Average per Month	April Plan	May Plan	June Plan	July Plan	August Plan	Year-end Total
INCOME											
Tuition	344,235	203,000	192,500	(10,500)	27,500	27,500	27,500	27,500	27,500	27,500	330,000
Fund-raising	3,500	2,042	1,000	(1,042)	143	0	0	1,000	0	0	2,000
County Grant	27,000	15,750	15,750	0	2,250	2,250	2,250	2,250	2,250	2,250	27,000
Other	2,000	1,167	992	(175)	142	142	142	142	142	142	1,701
TOTAL INCOME	376,735	221,959	210,242	(11,717)	30,035	29,892	29,892	30,892	29,892	29,892	360,701
EXPENSE											
Payroll Expense											
Salaries-Staff	270,000	157,241	158,033	(792)	22,576	21,236	21,236	21,236	21,236	21,236	264,213
Payroll Taxes	24,300	14,152	13,433	719	1,919	1,805	1,805	1,805	1,805	1,805	22,458
Worker's Comp	13,500	7,862	7,902	(40)	1,129	1,062	1,062	1,062	1,062	1,062	13,211
Staff Benefits											
Health Ins.	27,250	15,896	17,252	(1,356)	2,465	2,465	2,465	2,465	2,465	2,465	29,575
Dental Ins.	4,000	2,333	2,350	(17)	336	336	336	336	336	336	4,029
Education Allow.	875	510	585	(75)	84	84	84	84	84	84	1,003
Rent	4,800	2,800	2,800	0	400	400	400	400	400	400	4,800
Janitor	6,000	3,500	3,500	0	500	500	500	500	500	500	6,000
Insurance											
Liability	2,914	1,700	1,700	0	243	243	243	243	243	243	2,914
Accident	1,575	919	925	(6)	132	132	132	132	132	132	1,586
Directors Ins.	944	551	550	1	79	79	79	79	79	79	943
Supplies	15,000	8,750	6,540	2,210	934	934	934	934	934	934	11,211
Utilities	2,835	1,654	2,240	(586)	320	320	320	320	320	320	3,840
Capital Improvement	2,000	2,000	1,200	800	171	0	0	0	0	0	1,200
TOTAL EXPENSES	375,993	219,868	219,010	858	31,287	29,595	29,595	29,595	29,595	29,595	366,983
SURPLUS (DEFICIT)	742	2,091	(8,768)	(10,859)	(1,252)	297	297	1,297	297	297	(6,282)

Customize this form from the enclosed CD!

FIGURE 5–15 Felton Family Preschool Example 2: Further Cost Savings

Felton Family Preschool

Example 2: Final Plan—Deficit Reduction

	"Reasonable" Budget A3	Sept–March Budget	Sept–March Actual	Sept–March Variance	Average per Month	April Plan	May Plan	June Plan	July Plan	August Plan	Year-end Total
INCOME											
Tuition	344,235	203,000	192,500	(10,500)	27,500	27,500	27,500	27,500	27,500	27,500	330,000
Fund-raising	3,500	2,042	1,000	(1,042)	143	0	0	1,000	0	0	2,000
County Grant	27,000	15,750	15,750	0	2,250	2,250	2,250	2,250	2,250	2,250	27,000
Other	2,000	1,167	992	(175)	142	142	142	142	142	142	1,701
TOTAL INCOME	376,735	221,959	210,242	(11,717)	30,035	29,892	29,892	30,892	29,892	29,892	360,701
EXPENSE											
Payroll Expense											
Salaries-Staff	270,000	157,241	158,033	(792)	22,576	21,294	21,294	21,294	21,294	21,294	264,503
Payroll Taxes	24,300	14,152	13,433	719	1,919	1,810	1,810	1,810	1,810	1,810	22,483
Worker's Comp	13,500	7,862	7,902	(40)	1,129	1,065	1,065	1,065	1,065	1,065	13,227
Staff Benefits											
Health Ins.	27,250	15,896	17,252	(1,356)	2,465	2,465	2,465	2,465	2,465	2,465	29,577
Dental Ins.	4,000	2,333	2,350	(17)	336	336	336	336	336	336	4,030
Education Allow.	875	510	585	(75)	84	84	84	84	84	84	1,005
Rent	4,800	2,800	2,800	0	400	400	400	400	400	400	4,800
Janitor	6,000	3,500	3,500	0	500	500	500	500	500	500	6,000
Insurance											
Liability	2,914	1,700	1,700	0	243	243	243	243	243	243	2,915
Accident	1,575	919	925	(6)	132	132	132	132	132	132	1,585
Directors Ins.	944	551	550	1	79	79	79	79	79	79	945
Supplies	15,000	8,750	6,540	2,210	934	700	700	700	700	700	10,040
Utilities	2,835	1,654	2,240	(586)	320	119	119	119	119	119	2,835
Capital Improvement	2,000	2,000	1,200	800	171	0	0	0	0	0	1,200
TOTAL EXPENSES	375,993	219,868	219,010	858	31,288	29,227	29,227	29,227	29,227	29,227	365,145
SURPLUS (DEFICIT)	742	2,091	(8,768)	(10,859)	(1,253)	665	665	1,665	665	665	(4,444)

Customize this form from the enclosed CD!

FIGURE 5–16 Example 2: Final Plan for Reducing Deficit

Felton Family Preschool

Example 2: Alternative Plan—Deficit Reduction

	"Reasonable" Budget A3	Sept-March Budget	Sept-March Actual	Sept-March Variance	Average per Month	April Plan	May Plan	June Plan	July Plan	August Plan	Year-end Total
INCOME											
Tuition	344,235	203,000	192,500	(10,500)	27,500	27,500	27,500	27,500	27,500	27,500	330,000
Fund-raising	3,500	2,042	1,000	(1,042)	143	0	1,000	0	0	0	2,000
County Grant	27,000	15,750	15,750	0	2,250	2,250	2,250	2,250	2,250	2,250	27,000
Other	2,000	1,167	992	(175)	142	142	142	142	142	142	1,701
TOTAL INCOME	376,735	221,959	210,242	(11,717)	30,035	29,892	29,892	30,892	29,892	29,892	360,701
EXPENSE											
Payroll Expense											
Salaries-Staff	270,000	157,241	158,033	(792)	22,576	22,576	22,576	22,576	22,576	22,576	270,913
Payroll Taxes	24,300	14,152	13,433	719	1,919	1,919	1,919	1,919	1,919	1,919	23,028
Worker's Comp	13,500	7,862	7,902	(40)	1,129	1,129	1,129	1,129	1,129	1,129	13,546
Staff Benefits											
Health Ins.	27,250	15,896	17,252	(1,356)	2,465	2,465	2,465	2,465	2,465	2,465	29,575
Dental Ins.	4,000	2,333	2,350	(17)	336	336	336	336	336	336	4,029
Education Allow.	875	510	585	(75)	84	84	84	84	84	84	1,003
Rent	4,800	2,800	2,800	0	400	400	400	400	400	400	4,800
Janitor	6,000	3,500	3,500	0	500	500	500	500	500	500	6,000
Insurance											
Liability	2,914	1,700	1,700	0	243	243	243	243	243	243	2,914
Accident	1,575	919	925	(6)	132	132	132	132	132	132	1,586
Directors Ins.	944	551	550	1	79	79	79	79	79	79	943
Supplies	15,000	8,750	6,540	2,210	934	700	700	700	700	700	10,040
Utilities	2,835	1,654	2,240	(586)	320	119	119	119	119	119	2,835
Capital Improvement	2,000	2,000	1,200	800	171	0	0	0	0	0	1,200
TOTAL EXPENSES	375,993	219,868	219,010	858	31,287	30,680	30,680	30,680	30,680	30,680	372,411
SURPLUS (DEFICIT)	742	2,091	(8,768)	(10,859)	(1,253)	(788)	(788)	212	(788)	(788)	(11,710)

Customize this form from the enclosed CD!

FIGURE 5–17 Example 2: Alternative Plan for Deficit Reduction

per month, we may cut the supplies budget for the months of April through August to $700 per month.

Entering the new salary, utilities, and supplies cost figures into our worksheet, you can see in Figure 5–16, on page 98, that now the projected deficit at the end of our year has been reduced to about $4,400. Additional reductions have been realized in the expenses for payroll taxes and worker's compensation insurance as a result of the reduction in salaries.

If we decide we will not cut staffing at all because we do not want to have a negative impact on the quality of care in our classrooms, we may decide to maintain staffing levels as they are and only institute the other cost savings. Under this plan, we would end the year with a large deficit of $11,710. See Figure 5–17 on page 99. Significant savings are usually only found in the salary and benefit line items. No other variable cost category contains enough dollars.

Question 4: Can we increase enrollment or tuition fees during the next five months?   In a very small program or home child care business, increasing tuition revenue is probably the only possible solution to an operations deficit. This is because your largest expense item, your own salary, is most likely already at the minimum level you can afford. You may have to realize *less income in the short term*, but *in the longer term* you want to increase enrollment or fees so you can maintain a reasonable salary level. In larger child care centers, increasing enrollment and/or tuition fees may become part of the solution that evolves over the remainder of the year. If tuition revenue rises in the coming months and we expect it to stay at this higher level, we will be able to add back the hours we have taken away from some of the teachers. By keeping track of how we are doing every month we will know when we are able to make this decision.

THOUGHTS ON COST SAVINGS

The decision to realize cost savings through reductions in staffing is a very serious one. We all know the quality of care we provide in child care is directly related to the quality of our staff, which in turn is directly tied to their compensation. A full discussion of these considerations and how to maintain staff morale in times of cost cutting is presented in Chapter 3. I believe in compensating child care staff as fairly as possible, and, theoretically, I believe in charging the full cost of care for child care. But often in the real world we are faced with situations where in order to keep our program running, we may have to make cost savings through reducing staffing expenses. Each program will have to address these issues individually and make its own decisions. However, even though these are the hardest decisions to make, sometimes only reductions in staffing will provide the amount of savings needed to balance the budget. This is the only expense line item that has enough dollars in it to make a difference.

Rather than cutting hours from our regular staff, we can also look at cost savings in hiring substitutes. It might be possible, as we "staff only to enrollment," to eliminate some substitute hours when regular staff are absent. It is always preferable to trim staffing hours than to lay off employees, and to do it in a manner that is fair to all staff. As the Children's Center in Santa Cruz did, having staff involved in the decision-making process can not only help staff have some influence on the decisions that directly affect them, but the process can also generate new and innovative solutions that will provide cost savings with the least impact on staff and quality of care. Rather than give you the particular solutions for your own program's financial issues, this discussion illustrates ways of going about recognizing what the issues are and how to analyze what solutions to consider.

Our budget has thus become a useful planning tool as we proceed month to month through the fiscal year. This process is, however, only as good as the data we collect on actual operations. Let's explore how that is done in the next chapter.

Financial Record Keeping

THE REASONS WHY WE WANT TO KEEP GOOD FINANCIAL RECORDS

Our financial reports are only as good as the financial information we keep. For this reason alone we want to maintain the integrity of our financial data. But there are also other reasons for keeping accurate and timely financial records.

Legal Requirements

When we operate a business, we are required by law to keep certain financial records. It is not prescribed that we enter revenue and expenses daily, weekly, or in any particular format, but we are required to file tax returns, keep payroll records, and report to granting agencies information based on our financial records. In order to be able to prepare these legally mandated reports, we must have accurate financial information to report to these agencies.

In order to make our job easier, and to keep the tax and granting agencies happy, we want to have accurate and timely basic information about our revenue and expenses always readily accessible. This means we need more than a shoe box full of receipts and check stubs in our filing cabinet. It means we have recorded our spending and receiving of money in a consistent format and it is up to date within a week. It means the financial information can be read and understood by any agency that has given us money, is taxing us, and/or supervises our organization.

Required by Management

Usually the people who supervise us or who give us money want to know on occasion how we are doing financially. Most administrators are used to filing periodic financial reports to these interested parties. Boards of directors and corporate officers often request profit and

! TIP

Make a note on your calendar when reports are due for management and funding agencies and reminder notes approximately three weeks before due dates.

loss statements, sometimes called income statements, on a regular basis, either monthly or quarterly. Government agencies or foundations that have given us money for specific purposes will usually request information periodically throughout the course of the project and when the project is completed.

It is always easier to compile your financial information on a consistent, regular schedule than waiting for months and then trying to go back and recreate what happened. It is always better to record financial information when you are not rushed to meet a deadline. It is always better to be up to date on recording the basic financial information, so when you receive a last-minute request to prepare some type of financial report, you are able to respond immediately.

How It Helps You

If you are an administrator who came into the early childhood profession through your love of working with children and families, being a financial manager may not come easy. It probably is not your favorite part of the job of manager. But I do not believe you have to be a "numbers person" in order to be able to manage the finances of a child care organization. By understanding some basic bookkeeping and accounting techniques and using good accounting software, you can maintain accurate financial records, prepare financial reports, and actually understand what it all means. Through the process of keeping these financial records accurately and timely, you will gain a greater mastery of your organization's finances. You will also find the financial part of your job takes less of your time and is easier for you to do if you establish a schedule for yourself and do the finances on a regular, at least weekly, basis.

ACCRUAL VERSUS CASH BASIS OF ACCOUNTING

There are two basic ways to maintain financial records. You can record information on a **cash basis** or on an **accrual basis**. The difference between these two methods is that

- a cash system records income and expense when *cash comes in* or when *cash goes out* of your account(s);
- an accrual system records income and expense when that income item or expense item is *committed*.

Let's look at a couple of examples to clarify this difference.

Example 1: Tuition in the amount of $10,000 is billed on May 1. Families make payment over a 15-day period.

Day of Month	Cash System adds to tuition income	Accrual System adds to tuition income
May 1	$0	$10,000
May 5	$4,000	$0
May 10	$4,000	$0
May 15	$2,000	$0

Both systems record a total of $10,000 in tuition revenue for May. The accrual system records the entire amount on the billing day. The cash system only records the income as the payments are received and deposited. If, however, $1,500 was received and deposited on May 15 instead of $2,000, and no other payments were made in May, the cash system would record a total of $9,500 as May tuition income. The remaining $500 not paid is an **accounts receivable,** an amount that is still owed to you. Under the cash basis of accounting, an amount billed is never reported as income until the payment is received.

Example 2: An insurance bill in the amount of $6,000 for liability insurance for the coming fiscal year (July 1–June 30) is received on June 5 and paid in full on June 15.

Day of Month	Cash System	Accrual System
June 5 (month 1)	$0	$6,000 to prepaid insurance $6,000 to accounts payable
June 15	$6,000 to insurance exp. minus $6,000 from cash	minus $6,000 from cash and accounts payable
July 1	$0	minus $6,000/12 = $500 from prepaid insurance $500 charge to ins. expense
August 1	$0	minus prepaid ins. $500 $500 charge to ins. expense
September 1	$0	minus prepaid ins. $500 $500 charge to ins. expense
October 1	$0	minus prepaid ins. $500 $500 charge to ins. exp.

In this example there is a greater difference in the financial data recorded depending on which accounting system you use. Under the cash basis of accounting, an insurance expense in the amount of $6,000 is recorded all in the month of June. Your cash is reduced by the amount of the payment ($6,000) and your insurance expense is $6,000. Your financial results for this month will be highly skewed by this one entry. Under the accrual basis, the expense of $6,000, which pays for a 12-month insurance policy, is spread out evenly in $500 amounts for each month of the policy year. Although your cash has been reduced by the full amount of the insurance bill, the *expense* for insurance is equally distributed over the months during which the policy is in effect.

It is easier for very small businesses to maintain their records on a cash basis. Even midsize child care organizations can record their financial data on a cash basis unless they are required by corporate managers or boards to use the accrual system. At the end of your fiscal year, however, your accountant may convert your cash-basis numbers to accrual-basis numbers in preparing your year-end statements and tax returns. The accrual system is the generally accepted business accounting system that is recognized by most granting and taxing agencies. Adherence to generally accepted accounting principles (GAAP) may or may not be a requirement for your organization. Your accountant can answer this question.

! TIP

The accrual basis of accounting more accurately reflects the true costs of doing business month to month. It is the one method that is required for conformation to GAAP.

WHAT DOCUMENTS TO KEEP

A set of documents for recording financial information is essential for any size business. When you use computer accounting software, all of the necessary documents you need, plus many "extras," are included within the system. When you are keeping your own records manually or in spreadsheets you will need to maintain all of the following to provide a complete set of financial data.

Check Register

A check register contains financial information about spending and receiving money. It is the same thing you keep for your personal checking account. You can maintain this information in a handwritten ledger, in a computer spreadsheet, or within an accounting software package. Each line in the register represents one check you have written or one deposit you have made and should record the following:

date of check or deposit

payee name

check number

if not a check, whether it is a deposit or EFT (electronic funds transfer)

dollar amount of check or deposit

account to which the entry should be recorded

running account balance

and any memo, or note, regarding the entry

Figure 6–1 is an example of a spreadsheet to track money spent and deposits made for the Felton Family Preschool.

Since this document contains most of the day-to-day information about what is happening with your organization's money, it is the storeroom of data from which most of the other documents are derived. A separate check register should be kept for each bank account you own.

Bank Statements and Bank Reconciliation

At the end of every month, your bank sends you a bank statement for each of your bank accounts. You may receive this information online. Within a week of receiving these statements, it is important to reconcile your bank statement balance with the balance you have recorded on your check register. In other words, you want to verify that the amount of money the bank says you have in your account(s) is the same amount as is shown in your records. You want to be sure you have recorded accurately every transaction of funds coming into or leaving your account(s). Only after you have reconciled the monthly bank statement can you **close** the accounting month and prepare your monthly financial statements. Once the month is closed, no further transactions should be dated for that month. If errors in the month are discovered later on, the corrections can be entered in your system using the current date.

Bank reconciliation is a simple process. Accounting software programs take you through the same steps you need to take whether you use spreadsheets or a manual ledger. At month end, the bank balance you see in your computer or on your ledger will usually be different from the balance that your bank shows on their statement. They are different because you have written checks and deducted these amounts from your balance but the checks have not **cleared,** or passed through, the bank so they are not deducted from the bank's balance. The balances may also differ because you have made a deposit into the account that has not yet been recorded by the bank. For these reasons, the reconciliation process identifies what has and has not cleared through the bank. The bank statement balance will be adjusted for the uncleared items in order to compare it to your system's bank balance. In order to reconcile your bank account, follow these steps:

Step 1: Mark as cleared each check in your register that appears on the bank statement, verifying that the dollar amounts are the same.

Felton Family Preschool

Check Register

For the month of: _____

DATE	Payee Name	Deposit or Check #	Salaries-Staff	Staff Benefits	Payroll Tax	Rent	Janitor	Insurance	Supplies	Utilities	Capital Expense	Other	Deposits	Balance
														$8,745.12
6/1	Latifa	101	-1,039		-79.20									$7,626.72
6/1	Sheena	102	-617		-47.02									$6,962.66
6/1	Carol	103	-779		-59.40									$6,123.86
	ETC.													$6,123.86
														$6,123.86
6/5	ABC Building	104				-400.00								$5,723.86
6/5	Blue Cross	105		-2,269.40										$3,454.47
6/6	Blue Cross	106		-330.00										$3,124.47
6/10	State Fund Ins.	107		-550.25										$2,574.22
6/10	ABC Building	108					-500.00							$2,074.22
6/15	Lakeshore	109							-57.17					$2,017.05
6/12	Bank Deposit	DEP											3,715.10	$5,732.15
6/15	Bank Deposit	DEP											15,320.00	$21,052.15
	ETC													$21,052.15
														$21,052.15
	ETC													$21,052.15
														$21,052.15
														$21,052.15
														$21,052.15
														$21,052.15
														$21,052.15
TOTALS			-$2,435.63	-$3,149.65	-$185.62	-$400.00	-$500.00	$0.00	-$57.17	$0.00	$0.00	$0.00	19,035.10	$21,052.15

FIGURE 6–1 Felton Family Preschool Check Register

Customize this form from the enclosed CD!

Step 2: Mark as cleared all deposits in your register that appear on the bank statement, verifying that the dollar amounts are the same.

Step 3: Mark as cleared all other transactions, such as electronic funds transfers (EFTs) for bank service charges, payroll charges, etc., in your register that appear on the bank statement, verifying that the dollar amounts are the same.

Step 4: Draw a line under the last (latest date) transaction in your register that appears on the bank statement.

Step 5: Total all deposits and EFTs crediting the account with any funds that *have not* cleared through the bank account before this last transaction.

Step 6: Total all checks that *have not* yet cleared through the bank account.

Step 7: To the ending balance from the bank statement, add the total of deposits not cleared and subtract the total of checks not cleared. The result of this calculation should equal the account balance in your register.

If the amounts are equal, you have reconciled the account. In other words, if all the *uncleared* items had gone through the bank, the bank's balance would be the same as the account balance in your records. Attach your reconciliation computations to the month's bank statement and keep in a separate file for that bank account.

If the amounts are not the same, you have an error somewhere in your check register. There is no simple formula for finding errors. Some of the sources for these errors can be found if you ask yourself the following:

■ **Does the total of the checks cleared from your register plus any EFT withdrawals equal the total debits from your bank statement?** The total of all debits recorded by your bank for the month usually appears somewhere on your statement. If these totals are not equal, you have an error somewhere in one of the checks you entered. Again, verify the amounts of the checks in your register with the amounts recorded on your bank statement. Make sure you have recorded all of the EFT withdrawals in your check register.

■ **Does the total of deposits equal the total deposits credited to your account on the statement?** Again, your bank statement should contain a total for all deposits recorded that month. If they are not equal, your error is here somewhere. What is the amount of the difference? Look to see if this amount equals any deposit amounts on the bank statement or in your records.

If you have a manual or spreadsheet system, you may want to verify you have added and subtracted to the account balance accurately. Rerun the balance on an adding machine.

Income Register

Just as your check register details the information related to the spending of money, the income register details the information related to receiving money. This register should include:

■ the date of the receipt of funds

■ from whom the money was received

■ the check number

■ the amount of the receipt

■ the account name to which the money should be credited (tuition revenue, county grant, etc.)

! TIP

It is important that you reconcile all your bank accounts each month to detect any errors as soon as possible. You always want to know exactly how much money you have received, spent, and have remaining in your accounts.

	A	B	C	D	E	F	G	H	I	J
1										
2				Felton Family Preschool						
3				Income Register						
4										
5	For the month of: JUNE									
6										
7										
8	DATE	Received From	Check #	Tuition	Grant Funds	Fund-raising	Other	Deposits		
9										
10	6/3	Lopez	1118	300.00						
11	6/10	Jones	854	750.00						
12	6/11	Dubler	8050	400.00						
13	6/11	Lakeshore	109				15.10		refund for supplies	
14	6/11	County of SC	1154866		2250.00					
15	6/12	DEPOSIT MADE TO BANK						3715.10		
16										

FIGURE 6–2 Felton Family Preschool Income Register

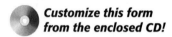

*Customize this form
from the enclosed CD!*

As funds are collected and deposited to your bank, an entry is made in this register of the total amount of the checks and cash deposited. For an example of a simple income register, see Figure 6–2.

Billing Records

Billing records for your families are most easily recorded in a spreadsheet or computer software application. If you are larger than a small family child care business, a manual system is too difficult to maintain and compile when you are preparing monthly and annual reports. You must record every bill to a family and every payment from the family. It is helpful to have the capability of preparing statements for families that display the charges and credits for a specified period of time.

In a child care home business, billing information can be recorded on ledger cards in a file box, or on pages in a loose-leaf notebook. With one card, or page, for each child, an entry is made for each bill, whether weekly, monthly, etc., and for each receipt of payment noting date of payment and check number. Sallie's Home Care has a system of large index cards in a file box. Each child's record is contained on one card. At the beginning of each year, Sallie will start a new card for each family and store the previous year's cards in a box labeled with that year. Figure 6–3 is one of the cards from Sallie's billing records.

Billing records for larger programs can be maintained along with all the information you track on enrolled children and wait-list children. Child care management software (see discussion below) usually does a good job of providing the database function along with the billing, or accounts receivable, function. Alternatively, you can maintain billing records for families in your accounting software or in spreadsheets (see Figure 6–4) that are separate from the database information on your children. If your billing is part of your accounting software, the recording of all your invoices and the receipt of payments from families will be incorporated in your other financial data. Under an accrual system, invoice amounts are recorded as income as of the date of the invoice and the amounts are also added to accounts receivable (the amounts owed to you). As payments from families are received, the payments reduce accounts receivables and add to your cash account. In Figure 6–4, as of June 11, which is the last date of the entries made, the Felton Preschool had billed a total of $28,370 for tuition, had received total payments of $21,500, and has an accounts receivable balance of $6,870 ($28,370 minus $21,500).

Sallie's Home Care Billing and Payment Ledger

Family Name: Bilter   Child's Name: Sam

9/1/03 full-time billed	800.00	
9/5/03 PAID		800.00	Ø
10/1/03 billed	800.00	
10/2/03 PAID		800.00	Ø
11/1/03 billed	800.00	
11/10/03 PAID		800.00	Ø

FIGURE 6–3 Sallie's Home Care Billing and Payment Ledger

	A	B	C	D	E	F	G
1							
2		**Felton Family Preschool**					
3		**Billed and Paid Tuition**					
4							
5	For the month of: JUNE						
6							
7	<u>DATE</u>	<u>Family Name</u>		<u>Tuition Billed</u>	<u>Tuition Paid</u>	<u>Balance</u>	
8							
9	6/1	Desai		$525.00			
10		Desai				$525.00	
11	6/1	Jones		$700.00			
12	6/10	Jones			$700.00	$0.00	
13	6/1	Dubler		$400.00			
14	6/11	Dubler			$400.00	$0.00	
15	6/1	Lopez		$370.00			
16	6/3	Lopez			$300.00	$70.00	
17	6/1	O'Neill		$650.00			
18		O'Neill				$650.00	
19	6/1	Jacobs		$650.00			
20		Jacobs				$650.00	
21							
22		ETC					
23							
24		ETC					
25							
26	6/1	Spode		$825.00			
27	6/2	Spode			$825.00		
28	6/1	Hersi		$825.00			
29	6/5	Hersi			$825.00		
30	6/1	Wcislo		$525.00			
31	6/1	Wcislo			$525.00		
32	6/1	Joseph		$600.00			
33	6/11	Joseph			$600.00		
34							
35	**TOTALS**			$28,370.00	$21,500.00	$6,870.00	
36							

FIGURE 6–4 Felton Family Preschool Billed
and Paid Tuition

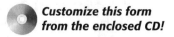
*Customize this form
from the enclosed CD!*

	A	B	C	D	E	F	G	H	I	J	K	L	M
1													
2							**Sallie's Home Care**						
3							**Payroll Register**						
4													
5													
6													
7	DATE	Employee	Hours	Rate	Gross Wages	FICA	Medicare	Federal WH	State WH	SDI	Net Wages	Check #	
8													
9	10/15	Sallie	80.00	$13.50	$1,080.00	67.50	2.70	86.40	54.00	1.08	$868.32	129	
10	10/15	Beth	60.00	$10.15	$609.00	38.06	1.52	48.72	30.45	0.61	$489.64	130	
11	10/31	Sallie	80.00	$13.50	$1,080.00	67.50	2.70	86.40	54.00	1.08	$868.32	139	
12	10/31	Beth	48.00	$10.15	$487.20	30.45	1.22	38.98	24.36	0.49	$391.71	140	
13	11/15	Sallie	80.00	$13.50	$1,080.00	67.50	2.70	86.40	54.00	1.08	$868.32	153	
14	11/15	Beth	50.00	$10.15	$507.50	31.72	1.27	40.60	25.38	0.51	$408.03	154	
15	11/30	Sallie	80.00	$13.50	$1,080.00	67.50	2.70	86.40	54.00	1.08	$868.32	166	
16	11/30	Beth	60.00	$10.15	$609.00	38.06	1.52	48.72	30.45	0.61	$489.64	167	
17	12/15	Sallie	80.00	$13.50	$1,080.00	67.50	2.70	86.40	54.00	1.08	$868.32	173	
18	12/15	Beth	60.00	$10.15	$609.00	38.06	1.52	48.72	30.45	0.61	$489.64	174	
19	12/31	Sallie	80.00	$13.50	$1,080.00	67.50	2.70	86.40	54.00	1.08	$868.32	180	
20	12/31	Beth	60.00	$10.15	$609.00	38.06	1.52	48.72	30.45	0.61	$489.64	181	
21													
22													
23		Totals	818.00		$9,910.70	$619.42	$24.78	$792.86	$495.54	$9.91	$7,968.20		
24													

FIGURE 6–5 Sallie's Home Care Payroll Register

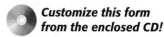

Customize this form from the enclosed CD!

! TIP

For business start-ups use the *Small Business Start-Up Kit* published by Nolo Press (Pakroo, 2000). It tells you all you need to know about business structures, governmental requirements, insurance, taxes, and hiring employees.

 Hint

Only if you are a very small agency should you consider maintaining your own payroll and payroll tax records. For a small fee, a payroll service or computer software company will do this for you.

Payroll Records

If you are paying only yourself and one or two other employees, it is possible to keep track of payroll records yourself. A sample payroll-recording register for Sallie's Home Care is shown in Figure 6–5. You must record any and all deductions from paychecks, including what you see in this chart: federal Social Security tax (FICA), Medicare tax, federal income tax withholding, state income tax withholding, and for some states, state disability tax or some additional local tax. All of these deductions are calculated as a percentage of the gross (total) wages. When you first register your business with the federal government (Internal Revenue Service), you will apply for an employer identification number, or EIN. You will receive booklets from the IRS and from your state government explaining how to withhold amounts from employees' paychecks and telling you when to remit these withheld amounts to each government agency.

You can begin to see the complexity of maintaining your own payroll records, understanding all the employer tax laws, and keeping track of what form and deposit to file and when to file. If you make a mistake, you will usually be responsible for interest and penalty fees. This is a job best left to organizations that specialize in payroll accounting. Computer accounting software will keep track of all of this for you and often will provide an additional service for a fee to produce the reports, pay the deposit, and file with the governing agency. Or you can pay a payroll service to do this job for you.

Profit and Loss Statement

A profit and loss (or income and expense) statement is the basic financial reporting document of all business entities. It displays, for the specified fiscal period of one week, one month, one quarter (one-fourth of one year, or three months), etc., what was earned, what

	A	B	C	D	E	F	G	H	I
1									
2			**Felton Family Preschool**						
3			Income and Expense Report						
4									
5								TOTAL	
6				June	July	August		Q4	
7									
8		INCOME							
9		Tuition		28,320	27,500	28,100		83,920	
10		Fund-raising		200	500	0		700	
11		County Grant		2,250	2,250	2,250		6,750	
12		Other		335	200	125		660	
13									
14		TOTAL INCOME		31,105	30,450	30,475		92,030	
15									
16		EXPENSE							
17		Payroll Expense							
18		Salaries-Staff		22,020	24,410	21,740		68,170	
19		Payroll Taxes		1,845	1,896	1,908		5,649	
20		Worker's Comp		1,101	1,220	1,087		3,408	
21		Staff Benefits							
22		Health Ins.		2,275	2,310	2,310		6,895	
23		Dental Ins.		303	350	350		1,003	
24		Education Allow.		0	110	0		110	
25		Rent		400	400	400		1,200	
26		Janitor		615	500	500		1,615	
27		Insurance							
28		Liability		245	245	245		735	
29		Accident		135	135	135		405	
30		Directors Ins.		85	85	85		255	
31		Supplies		542	175	1,000		1,717	
32		Utilities		180	174	166		520	
33									
34		Capital Improvement		0	0	0		0	
35		**TOTAL EXPENSES**		29,746	32,010	29,926		91,682	
36									
37		**SURPLUS (DEFICIT)**		1,359	(1,560)	549		348	
38									

FIGURE 6–6 Felton Family Preschool Income and Expense Report

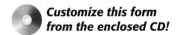

Customize this form from the enclosed CD!

was spent, and the net gain or loss. An income and expense report in Figure 6–6 shows the financial activity at the Felton Family Preschool for the months of June, July, and August, and adds the three months to display a quarterly total. This is the Felton school's fourth quarter, since its fiscal year extends from September 1 through August 31. The center had a surplus of $348 for these three months. The compilation of all the data that you have entered as invoices, checks, bills from vendors, and payroll expense, produces this statement. If you have accounting software, an income and expense report is produced with a few clicks of your mouse. If your system is manual or contained in computer spreadsheets, you will have to do the computations to add up the right numbers into the right categories.

Balance Sheet

The other basic financial reporting document in business is the balance sheet. Instead of showing the financial *activity* over a period of time as we see in the profit and loss statement, a balance sheet is a *snapshot* of your assets (what you own or what has been prepaid) and your liabilities (what you owe) at a particular point in time. A balance sheet is easily produced in accounting software. If you maintain your accounting records manually or in computer spreadsheets, it is advisable to seek professional help in preparing your balance sheet. In small- to midsize organizations you probably only need to prepare a balance sheet at the end of each fiscal year. The CPA who prepares your year-end tax reports can provide you with a year-end balance sheet. Instead of preparing a full balance sheet each month, you may want to produce a document that lists only your cash (bank) accounts and the balances in each account as of the end of the month. This information will be useful to you and your supervisors.

HOW TO KEEP YOUR FINANCIAL RECORDS

You have three basic choices of methods to use for tracking your financial information: a manual system (paper and pencil), a system of computer spreadsheets, or a computer accounting software package. In the following sections we will examine the suitability of each of these methods.

Manual Systems

Maintaining accurate financial records does not require a sophisticated computer system. For some very small facilities or child care homes, a manual bookkeeping system can work adequately. If, for example, you serve only six children, have no employees, and write ten or fewer expense checks per month, you can design a manual system to track your revenue and expenses. An example of a bookkeeping register for Sallie's Home Care is shown in Figure 6–7. At the end of each month, quarter, and year, the expense and revenue columns are totaled and manually transferred to an income and expense report. The figures from Figure 6–7 for the months of June, July, and August have been totaled and transferred to the report in Figure 6–8. Bills for families are prepared manually, or may be typed on a computer, and copies are kept for her records. As payments come in, an entry is made on the family's ledger card for the payment received. Sallie does not prepare a balance sheet.

The advantage of a manual system is its ease of use and low cost. All you really need is a pencil with a good eraser, a tablet of ledger paper, and a calculator. The downside of these simple systems, though, is that it is more difficult to prepare your financial reports: you have to manually add and transfer figures from your basic data. Each time you add a number or transfer it to a different piece of paper there is the possibility of making an error. If you have a larger volume of transactions, manual systems can also be much more time consuming than maintaining records on a computer. These are records that will make it so much easier to prepare your annual tax returns, whether you do them yourself or hire someone to do it.

Computer Spreadsheets

One step up from manual systems are financial record-keeping systems maintained in computer spreadsheets. I recommend this alternative only to someone who really enjoys building spreadsheets on a computer and who also has a clear understanding of accounting principles. It can be very time consuming to construct these documents initially, and to verify they are accurately recording the data you need. Spreadsheets are needed for the following:

> Check register: to record payments you make
>
> Income register: to record funds received and bank deposits made
>
> Weekly (or monthly) billing record: to record charges to families and payments received

Sallie's Home Care

Check Register

DATE	Payee Name	Deposit or Check#	Salaries-Staff	Payroll Tax	Insurance	Supplies	Maintenance	Utilities	Capital Expense	Deposits	Balance
6/1	Beginning Balance										$2,746.29
											$2,746.29
6/1	Sallie	215	-$1,080.00	$211.68							$1,877.97
6/1	Beth	216	-$507.50	$99.47							$1,469.94
6/11	Lakeshore	217				-$112.15					$1,357.79
6/15	Tuition Paid									$4,470.00	$5,827.79
6/15	Sallie	218	-$1,080.00	$211.68							$4,959.47
6/15	Beth	219	-$487.20	$95.49							$4,567.76
6/20	State Fund	220			-$170.00						$4,397.76
6/20	Holder, Babbit	221			-$75.00						$4,322.76
6/20	PG&E	222						-$47.36			$4,275.40
7/1	Sallie	223	-$1,080.00	$211.68							$3,407.08
7/1	Beth	224	-$487.20	$95.49							$3,015.37
7/1	Delmar Roofing	225					-$475.00				$2,540.37
7/12	Tuition Paid									$4,020.00	$6,560.37
7/13	Sallie	226	-$1,080.00	$211.68							$5,692.05
7/15	Beth	227	-$487.20	$95.49							$5,300.34
7/20	State Fund	228			-$154.00						$5,146.34
7/20	Holder, Babbit	229			-$75.00						$5,071.34
7/20	PG&E	230						-$45.50			$5,025.84
8/1	Sallie	231	-$1,080.00	$211.68							$4,157.52
8/15	Sallie	232	-$1,080.00	$211.68							$3,289.20
8/20	State Fund	233			-$115.00						$3,174.20
8/20	Holder, Babbit	234			-$75.00						$3,099.20
8/20	PG&E	235						-$35.41			$3,063.79
8/31	I.R.S.	236	-$1,829.00								$1,234.79
8/31	CA Emply. Develop.	237	-$465.00								$769.79
TOTALS			-$8,449.10	-$637.98	-$664.00	-$112.15	-$475.00	-$128.27	$0.00	$8,490.00	

FIGURE 6–7 Sallie's Home Care Check Register

Customize this form from the enclosed CD!

Sallie's Home Care

Profit and Loss Report

	June	July	August	Total Q4
INCOME				
Tuition	4,470	4,020	0	8,490
Fund-raising	0	0	0	0
TOTAL INCOME	4,470	4,020	0	8,490
EXPENSE				
Payroll Expense				
Salaries-Staff	3,155	3,134	2,160	8,499
Payroll Taxes	(618)	(614)	1,871	639
Worker's Comp	170	154	115	439
Insurance				
Liability & Accident	75	75	75	225
Supplies	112	0	0	112
Maintenance	0	475	0	475
Utilities	47	46	35	128
Capital Expense	0	0	0	0
TOTAL EXPENSES	2,941	3,270	4,256	10,467
SURPLUS (DEFICIT)	1,529	750	(4,256)	(1,977)

FIGURE 6–8 Sallie's Home Care Fourth Quarter Profit and Loss Report

Payroll register: to keep track of payroll if you prepare your own payroll checks

Profit and loss statement: to display, for the time period specified, how much money was received and how much money was spent

Samples of these documents appear in Figures 6–1 and 6–2, and in Figures 6–4 through 6–6.

Unless you have less than four employees, I do not recommend preparing your own paychecks. It can be complicated when you are also preparing employer tax reports and making monthly or quarterly tax payments. Outside services such as PayChex® and ADP® do an excellent job for even a small organization, and the cost of this kind of service is very reasonable. You won't have to worry about keeping up with changes to employer tax laws or remembering the date payments are due. This is all the payroll service does, and it can do a much better job than you.

Computer Software

For any child care organization larger than a family child care home or a one-room school, a computer software program to maintain your financial records should be used. You do not have to be an accountant or financial wizard to use such programs. You enter the basic financial data and the software organizes the data and stores it. The program puts the income data into the proper place when you record a payment by a family, and puts the expense information where it should go when you enter the information for a check you are writing. There are usually standard formats in these systems for all kinds of reports and for bills to customers. Some software systems allow you to create your own (customize) formats for reports and invoices. Some systems give you a choice among a few built-in formats. The financial information is automatically organized and combined for time periods you specify. The data is always readily available to you in several different formats you designate.

It is best to introduce new software to your organization at the beginning of a fiscal year. If you do so, it is not necessary to transfer all of the current year's transactions from the old system. You will only have to enter data for accounts that have to carry forward to the new year, such as bank account balances and customer account balances. The ideal way to start a new system is to maintain your old accounting system and use your new system in parallel for about a month. It does mean entering all of the financial data into both systems for this period of time, but it is a way to test and verify your new system is working and producing the same results as your current system. It may actually uncover flaws in the system you are currently using.

Child Care Management Software.   I have not yet found a child care management software product that does an adequate job in recording financial information. My experience with these products has taught me that child care software developers do not really understand accounting principles. They do a good job of recording and organizing all the information we need to maintain on the families and children in our programs; in other words, child care management programs are usually good database systems. But so far, they have not done an adequate job of recording accounting data and preparing financial reports. This situation can change, however, so it may be worth your time to talk with other administrators about their experience with child care management software and even test a few of them in your own environment. If you are working for a corporate child care program or in a program like Head Start, the computer software you will be using is chosen by someone else and you may have to learn how to work around a software system that doesn't exactly do what you want it to do.

Accounting Software.   The best systems for maintaining financial records on a computer are accounting software programs. There are many programs on the market you can use. Some are more complicated than others and some are more adaptable to child care finances than others. The best accounting software system I have found—and which I have used in several child care programs—is QuickBooks®. This software is available for PCs and Macintosh computers. It is a very good investment of about $200 to $300. When upgrades are published, you can purchase them for a lot less than the initial purchase of the software. On installing the upgrade, all your financial data is automatically transferred to the new system.

If you are a PC user, there are many other accounting software packages you can choose. Accounting software called My Bookkeeper® sells for $30 and offers a $10 mail-in rebate. It looks much like QuickBooks® in the design of its screens and the way information is organized. It includes all of the functions a small center or school would need: billing, payroll, a chart of accounts, financial reports, bill paying, and an online help feature. There is only one chart of accounts in the system. You can delete some of the accounts included, but you cannot add your own-named accounts to the list. My Bookkeeper® allows you to add customized information to your customer records, so that, for example, you could add information for the child's name, birthday, and schedule. A step up from My

Bookkeeper®, but still less expensive than QuickBooks®, is Peachtree First Accounting®. Usually selling for about $100, Peachtree® offers most of the same features as QuickBooks®. It starts you out with a guided tour of how the system works, and walks you through entering initial information in its setup guide. Peachtree® includes 75 sample companies from which you can choose the one most like your business and use their chart of accounts.

Using Your Accounting Software.   Once you have purchased accounting software and installed it on your computer, take some time to browse through the different parts or modules included in it. Find a quiet time when you can spend an hour going through the on-line tutorial. QuickBooks® includes an interactive interview when you first set up your organization. It takes you step by step through all the necessary sections where you enter information about your center: general information about your organization, your chart of accounts, and accounting specific information.

Your chart of accounts can be modified at any time. By a click of your mouse you can add, edit, delete, or rearrange the order of any of the accounts in your chart. You can create subaccounts where you may want to record more detailed information. For example, you may have an expense account for payroll costs that is made up of several subaccounts for teacher salaries, office salaries, substitute salaries, payroll taxes, staff benefits, and worker's compensation insurance. You may have several income subaccounts: tuition fees, county grant funds, donations, and interest on investments.

Once you have established the basic company information and the chart of accounts, you will probably want to enter additional information. Your accounting software probably maintains lists for the following:

customers (your families and children)

vendors (businesses you buy from)

items (the services you sell)

employees

Chart of Accounts

The chart of accounts for your organization is a very important document. It defines how your financial information is stored, organized, and reported. By being thoughtful in designing your chart of accounts, you will find the financial information coming out of your system is exactly the information you and your management need to understand how your organization is functioning financially and how to strategize to reverse financial weaknesses.

A chart of accounts is merely a listing of all the separate categories in which financial information is stored and reported. Every organization has assets—i.e., things you *own*, such as bank accounts or furniture, and things for which you have prepaid, such as insurance paid for a 12-month period in the future—and liabilities, or things you *owe*. Assets and liabilities can be current or long term. A current asset is one that is either cash or can be readily transformed into cash. A current liability is one that is due, or owed, within one year or less. You always want to have more assets than liabilities.

You will also set up accounts in the chart of accounts for all your income categories and all your expense categories. These accounts allow you to keep track of the categories of income received and money spent. A very simple chart of accounts for the Felton Family Preschool appears in Figure 6–9. Figure 6–10 displays a more elaborate chart of accounts.

Felton Family Preschool

Chart of Accounts

ASSETS

Current Assets
    Cash
    Accounts Receivable
Fixed Assets

LIABILITIES

Current Liabilities
    Accounts Payable
    Other Current Liabilities

EQUITY

INCOME ACCOUNTS

Tuition and Fees
Other Income

EXPENSE ACCOUNTS

Salaries-Staff
Staff Benefits
Payroll Taxes
Rent
Janitor
Insurance
Supplies
Utilities
Capital Expense
Other Expense

FIGURE 6–9 Felton Family Preschool Chart of Accounts

Paying bills becomes a simple process. You can enter bill information filling in the date, payee, amount, and account to be charged for that expense. You can enter bills as they are received in your office, then pay them at a later date, or pay them as bills are entered.

Most accounting software programs will include a payroll function. You can create your own paychecks and file your own payroll taxes and employer reports. Alternatively, you could send your payroll data to an outside payroll service, and then you only have to enter into your accounting records the total dollar amounts that come out of your bank account to pay staff and the dollar amounts of payroll taxes paid. The benefit of incorporating payroll into your accounting software is you then have the capability of analyzing staffing costs and preparing reports about your payroll expenses. You can make immediate changes, additions,

---

Felton Family Preschool

Chart of Accounts II

ASSETS

Current Assets
- Checking Account
- Restricted Fund Account
- Construction Account
- Accounts Receivable

Fixed Assets
- Office Equipment
- Furniture

LIABILITIES

Current Liabilities
- Accounts Payable Payroll Liability
- Tax Liability
- Credit Card
- Other Current Liabilities

Long-term Liabilities

EQUITY

INCOME ACCOUNTS

Tuition

Fund-raising

Donations

County Grant

Food Program

Interest Income

Other Income

EXPENSE ACCOUNTS

Salaries-Teaching Staff

Salaries-Administrative Staff

Salaries-Substitute Teachers

Staff Benefits
- Health Insurance
- Dental Insurance
- Education Allowance
- Payroll Taxes
- Worker's Comp Insurance

Rent

Janitor
- Cleaning
- Maintenance and Repair

Insurance
- Liability
- Accident
- Director's Liability

Supplies
- Center Supplies
- Classroom Supplies
  - Toddler Room
  - Young Preschool Room
  - Preschool Room
- Health Supplies
- Office Supplies

Utilities

Capital Expense

Other Expense

FIGURE 6–10 Felton Family Preschool Chart of Accounts II

and deletions to your list of employees. You also avoid the possibility of making an error when you transfer payroll amounts into your computer from an outside vendor.

A bank account reconciliation feature should be included in good accounting software. In QuickBooks® this function is especially well organized and straightforward. With your bank statement in front of you, you can read the checks and deposits on the QuickBooks® screen and check off each item that appears (or has cleared) on your statement. At the bottom of the screen, QuickBooks® tells you whether you are in balance, or if you are not, how much the difference is. You can leave this screen to go into your check register to find the error and all the data you have cleared will stay cleared. You can return to the reconcile process immediately or return a few days later. Once the account is balanced, you can produce a reconciliation report for each account.

It is good accounting practice to close each accounting period (i.e., each month). Thus, once the month ends and you have made all the entries that should be in that month and have reconciled the bank statement, *no further entries* are made using that month's date. Corrections are made in the current month only, with a reference to the date of the original transaction. By following this procedure carefully, you will avoid changing previous months' financial data that has already been reported.

For example, if I have closed the month of November and have prepared and distributed all my financial reports for that month and have reconciled the bank statement ending November 30, I do not want to enter any other transactions with a November date. If I discover, say on January 3, that a check dated in November has been lost, I will make a reversing entry dated January 3 to credit whatever expense account had been charged and to add back the check amount into my bank account.

Entering budget data into your accounting system is another valuable function. You want to be able to enter budget amounts line by line for each category of income and expense. A total for each line should be computed so that you can verify that the monthly amounts you have just entered total to the correct annual figure. When it comes time to produce your monthly financial reports you want to be able to produce reports that compare actual results to budget estimates as we did in Chapter 5. For example, a budget report for September can display a column for September actuals, a column for September budget amounts, and columns for the dollar variance and percent variance for each line.

> **! TIP**
>
> An accounting entry should never be made in a past month that has already been closed.

FISCAL YEAR-END

Unless you are a very small program or have a corporate or head office that takes care of financial reporting and tax returns, you will want to hire a certified public accountant (CPA) at the end of your fiscal year. If you are a nonprofit organization, look for an accountant specializing in small, nonprofit organizations, because the laws governing nonprofits are different from the laws for other organizations. Check with colleagues who may be able to recommend a good accountant. Call a few out of the phone book and meet with them until you find one with whom you are comfortable. Make sure you understand what your accountant is talking about. It does not help you if your accountant only speaks accounting jargon and never really seems to understand what *your* issues are.

Your accountant should prepare your year-end profit and loss statement, your year-end balance sheet, and your year-end tax returns. In addition, a good accountant will recommend any changes in your procedures that he feels are warranted. A good accountant is available to you by phone to answer your financial questions.

FINANCIAL RECORD KEEPING 101

Congratulations! You have just completed your first basic accounting class. As you become more familiar with the financial record-keeping system of your organization, it will become easier to stay up to date on this information. It will start to take less of your time each month. The financial information will now be at your fingertips when you need to produce a report for someone, or analyze why, for example, your payroll costs are running too high. Each month you will know whether your program made or lost money and whether tuition revenue is high enough to cover the costs of doing business. You will find that in addition to having more time to focus on other aspects of your job, you will have more mental energy to do so because you now have confidence in the financial status of your organization.

REFERENCE

Pakroo, P. H. (2000). *The Small Business Start-Up Kit.* (2nd ed.) Berkeley, CA: Nolo Press.

The Decision-Making Process

WHO IS MAKING THE DECISIONS?

There is one final topic for you to consider as a child care administrator. In all that we have discussed so far someone is responsible for making decisions, whether it is about capacity, ratios, whom to hire, when to order supplies, or what tuition rate increase to recommend. We should be mindful about who is making these decisions and how they are made.

Administrator's Role in Decision Making

I am sure that in your job as a child care administrator you make many decisions every day without thinking much about it. By the time it is the lunch hour you probably have had to decide whether to call in a substitute teacher for one of your regular teachers who called in sick that morning, what to say to a parent who has been consistently 10 to 20 minutes late picking up her child at closing time, when to set up your next staff meeting, and what you are going to tell a teacher about her request for time off. Making decisions is integral to the job of child care manager, so learning more about this process and how to be more successful at it is worth your time.

The first and most important thing to learn is you cannot and should not make *all* the decisions for *everyone* at the center. If you try to do so, you will find that you get nothing else done. Teachers will learn to rely on you for the answer to every little question. You will be faced with constant interruptions. Some administrators may unintentionally want to be the only one making decisions in their organization. It is a way of proving their worth, of showing how they are the only ones capable of keeping the business running. All too soon, however, this kind of administrator will find herself overwhelmed by trivial decision making with no time left for the really important decisions that only she can make.

! **TIP**

You should never be the only decision maker in your organization. Your worth as the leader of an organization is based on how well you can lead others and train them to make their own decisions.

If you make all the decisions for all of your staff, you are teaching them they are not capable of making their own decisions. You are essentially saying to them, "You must come to me to answer all your questions and make all your choices because obviously I will know what to do and you do not know what to do." They will never gain the experience of making informed decisions. It takes much less of their effort to go into your office and ask for your solution.

Instead of making all the decisions, your goal should be to make the *fewest* decisions yourself. Your staff should be making most of the day-to-day decisions concerning the program in their classroom: how the dishwasher gets loaded, when to serve snack. The classroom team should be able to figure out when they need an additional teacher in their room for adequate coverage. Your goal is to train staff so they are capable of making these kinds of decisions, not only because it frees up your time, but also because it empowers the teachers to control their immediate environment. They are the closest to what is needed in the classroom, they are the ones who have the most information on which to base a decision, and they are the ones who will be most affected by the outcome of the decision.

This does not mean, however, that you make no decisions. Don't worry. There are lots of decisions that will have to be left to you. The child care administrator usually makes those decisions that will affect the whole organization, such as hiring decisions and decisions about budgets and spending money. You will be making decisions about paying staff and how to recruit new teachers to your center. And, sometimes, when a classroom teacher comes to you because she has decided she will need another staff member to help cover the lunch hour, you may decide the teaching team will have to cope with the staff they have.

The Role of Your Staff in Decision Making

Helping teachers and office staff in your school get into the habit of making their own decisions should be an important priority. The more others are able to think for themselves, the more time you have available to focus on those things only you can do. When teachers come to you for answers, turn the question back to them. Let them know you trust them and that they can resolve the problem on their own. For some staff, you may need to start out with small issues until they feel more confident. As they become more competent at making decisions, they will be able to tackle larger problems. For other staff you may need to be watchful they do not step into your area of decision making. Some staff may need clear guidelines as to what is and is not their responsibility.

Teachers may make mistakes when they decide an issue; this is all part of the process of learning how to make decisions. The mistakes will most likely not be critical. Most decisions can be overturned if we see they are not working. A new choice is then made and we can evaluate how our new approach is working. We are used to doing this all the time when we problem solve about children's behavior. Your staff will learn a lot from their mistakes and this will help them make better decisions in the future. And when they really get stuck after trying to find a solution, they will come to you and you will then be able to help them work through other possible options.

Modeling good decision making to your staff allows them to learn from watching you. By encouraging the dissemination of center information and being open about the choices you are making, it will become more obvious to others how you make decisions. Staff will observe you collecting and sifting through information that helps you form your decisions. They will often be involved in preliminary discussions where they see you are considering many sides of a problem. And, once you make a decision, it will be much more obvious to others how you have arrived at that course of action. When you find you have made a mistake, don't be afraid to admit it. This is good modeling, too. Your mistake has probably not been a complete disaster; you can work on finding an alternate solution.

WHAT IS INCLUSIVE DECISION MAKING?

The kind of decision making that I am talking about, and which has been described in many of the examples in this book, I call **inclusive decision making.** It is where others are *included* in the decision-making process. Although it is similar to decision making by consensus, it is not the same thing. A decision made by consensus is a decision where there is "general agreement among all the members of a group" (*Webster's New Collegiate Dictionary,* 1980 p. 238). As shall become clearer as we explore some examples of the process, inclusive decision making does not necessarily guarantee general agreement among all group members.

The decision-making process can look different in different child care organizations. And it should. It is important in all organizations to make whatever process you use clear to all staff members by writing it down, posting it for your staff to read, and maybe including it in the staff handbook. (See the box below for one example developed by the staff at the Felton Family Preschool.) Perhaps you want to involve the whole organization in the design of your center's decision-making process. You want each individual to be clear about their own role in the process each time a decision is being made, e.g., whether they are a participant in the information gathering and crafting of a solution, or whether they are the ultimate decision maker at the end of the process.

Inclusive Decision Making in a Child Care Environment

Inclusive decision making in child care can take place on many levels. Within each classroom, a teaching team can be responsible for the many decisions that must be made in order to provide quality care for a particular group of children. Through team meetings, the teachers can discuss such responsibilities as their daily schedule, the needs of the individual and group of children in their care and the activities they want to plan for the children, the primary care

The Decision Process for the Felton Family Preschool

I. Idea/Proposal generated or a problem is identified.

II. Decide whether a group process is needed or one decision maker.

III. For a group process, identify and name who will be responsible for the final decision: an individual; a group, by majority vote; or everyone, by unanimous consent.

IV. By general agreement, set a time limit for discussion(s).

V. Discuss.

VI. Close discussion.

VII. Clarify and write out a proposal or solution.

VIII. Poll the group. (By a show of hands, determine who is in favor of solution.)

IX. If unanimous decision is required, but the group is not in full agreement, vote to decide whether discussion will continue or whether more information gathering is needed.

X. If one decision maker is responsible, that person decides whether further work is needed or whether she has enough information to make her decision.

XI. Process circles back to Step V until a decision can be reached.

groups for each teacher, and how classroom jobs are distributed among staff each day, each week. In order to make informed decisions some information may first need to be gathered, then assessed. Other responsibilities, such as classroom jobs, can be assigned by an agreement among the teachers. On some occasions, the head teacher may need to assign tasks if general agreement cannot be reached. She will often have the final authority to make decisions, or change decisions, that affect the classroom.

Other kinds of decisions can be made by groups of staff members that are brought together for the sole purpose of making a specific decision or set of decisions. For example, our center celebrated the Week of the Young Child each April. A volunteer committee made up of members of our staff was formed to work on this event. Their responsibilities included raising money for the event, planning celebration activities throughout the week, and organizing a family festival. As director, I was kept informed of the committee's progress and plans. But other than having a very peripheral role, I was not involved in their work. My only specific directions to the committee were raise enough money to pay for the event and plan a festival for families on the final Saturday. Committee members made all their own decisions. The Week of the Young Child celebration became an event for which we always had eager volunteers, and to which we all looked forward each year. Committee members understood their roles and felt responsible for the results of their own planning. They took over a huge job that otherwise would have been one more thing for me to do.

Effect on the Community

✓ Hint

Inclusive decision making helps to create a positive organizational climate.

One of the reasons I am such a strong proponent of using inclusive decision making is that it has a strong positive effect on the climate of any organization. The process may not always produce the "best" results. It usually takes longer to reach a decision by a group process. There is no guarantee that everyone will be happy with the results. It doesn't mean that there will never be any mistakes made. But it does mean that your staff and your parents will be involved in your program and will know that they are a central part of what happens there. They will know their voices are heard and they can make a difference in how the program operates. There will be fewer secrets and fewer rumors circulating through the center based on incomplete or erroneous information. And there will be a true basis on which to build trust within your community.

WHAT INCLUSIVE DECISION MAKING LOOKS LIKE: FOUR EXAMPLES

Hiring a Teacher

A full description of the inclusion-based process of hiring a new teacher is included in Chapter 3, in the section titled "Hiring."

Budgets

If you are responsible for preparing the budget for your program, you may never have considered sharing this responsibility with others in your organization. I think it is the only way to prepare a budget. By incorporating the expertise of the teachers and administrative staff as well as your supervisor(s) or board members, you will be able to build a budget that more closely reflects your program. You will also have buy-in from your community about the rates you set for tuition fees, the fund-raising you plan to do, and how you plan to spend money.

On the cost side of budget planning, I solicited input from my program coordinators on salary recommendations for the teachers in their program. I provided details on hours and rates of pay of each teacher in their program. Sometimes I gave the coordinators a percentage range for salary increases (say, between 2 percent and 4 percent) and a total not-to-exceed dollar amount of an increase that they could distribute among the staff in their program. Each coordinator, in discussions with me, then determined the specific amount of increase to give each individual teacher.

Other staff were involved in planning budget amounts for classroom and outdoor supplies and for any unusually large expense that would be required for a capital improvement project. Teaching teams met to discuss their plans for the coming year to determine what expenses they were planning. My administrative team, too, discussed things we'd like to see happen in the coming year. We made a wish list of new endeavors and attached a dollar value to each. Then we attempted to prioritize this list. As we got closer to developing a final budget, we could see which of these items we could "fit" into the budget, working down the list from our first priority.

Every year our board of directors reviewed my recommendations for changes to tuition fees. Often I presented more than one proposal. They gave me feedback from a parent's perspective when they felt increases were too high, or whether they believed any increase should be considered at all. In full board meetings, or meeting with the finance committee, we hammered out a final plan. The final decision on rates was always determined by a vote of the board.

Performance Reviews

The performance review process already described in Chapter 3 is another good example of inclusive decision making. Both the employee being reviewed and the supervisor conducting the review have shared decision-making authority in deciding the performance goals to be articulated. Before the review meeting takes place, each employee receives a form to complete that encourages her to begin thinking about the review process. A sample format from *Blueprint for Action* with teacher Teresa's responses appears in Figure 7–1 (Bloom, p. 267). The completed form is brought into the conference along with any documentation she may bring of her accomplishments over the past year. You will also, hopefully, have notes you have made for each staff member over the year, giving details about specific areas of strength you have observed and areas where more training may be required. Figure 7–2 shows some sample notes that were collected regarding Teresa's work in the preschool room. These are discussed and reformatted into a listing of the teacher's

- strengths
- areas needing improvement
- listing of goals and objectives

in Figure 7–3 (adapted from Bloom, p. 268).

Teresa is actively involved in her own evaluation through the development of her individual goals and objectives and through the discussion that takes place between her and her supervisor. Once a clear set of objectives has been determined, employee and supervisor can map out a plan of activities to be scheduled to help Teresa accomplish her goals. It is a plan that will be revisited during the year. At these subsequent reviews, teacher and supervisor can determine how well Teresa has been able to follow the original plan and whether any modifications should be considered in the list of activities or the timing of these activities.

Moving Children

Many child care programs move children into the next age group as they are developmentally ready. In our large center of nine classrooms, we moved whole classrooms of children at the beginning of each school year in September. Our usual procedure did not prevent us from

Staff Pre-Conference Questionnaire

Dear *Teresa*

As you prepare for our planning conference, think about the following:

■ What aspect of your job gives you the greatest personal satisfaction?

Love the kids & families!

■ What aspect of your job is most frustrating?

Early shift.

■ What keeps you from being as effective as you would like to be in your position?

Nothing.

■ If you had the power to change anything about your job, what would you change? Why would this be an improvement over existing conditions?

Have a later shift then I could get here on time.

■ What do you see yourself doing five years from now?

Working here.

■ What new skills or knowledge would you like to learn next year?

Science & language activities for 2s.

■ How can I or other staff help you achieve your personal and professional goals?

Pay me more! Provide workshop on 2-year-old curriculum.

FIGURE 7–1 Staff Pre-Conference Questionnaire

File Notes

Teresa

Date	Observation
10/4/02	Helping child w. potty accident. –calm, no blaming, matter-of-fact.
11/7/02	Late for opening shift all week—spoke to her about it.
11/20/02	Better at arriving on time—seems to be making an effort. Some trouble keeping breaks within time limit.
12/10/02	Little innovation in creating curriculum for youngest children. May suggest she meet with mentor teacher to brainstorm some new ideas.
1/29/03	Little progress in curriculum development.
3/20/03	Consistently cheerful attitude when asked to help out in other classrooms. Seems to get on well with other staff and kids. Knows many of our families at center.

FIGURE 7–2 File Notes for Staff Review

Goals Planning

Name of Teacher _Teresa B._   Date _5-10-03_

Your strengths in the classroom:

1. _Relationship building with children._

2. _Relationship building with parents._

3. _Willingness to help wherever needed._

Your areas for improvement:

1. _New curriculum ideas._

2. _Being consistently on time._

3. _____

Your objectives for the year ahead:

1. _Attend a curriculum workshop for 2s._

2. _Enroll in and complete an ECE class in literacy._

3. _Be on time for morning shift._

Supervisor signature _Mr. Director_   Date: _5-10-03_

FIGURE 7–3 Goals Planning Template

moving children on occasion when it was necessary to do so. But most of our children stayed in the same room for one or two years, then moved with their classmates in September to an older classroom.

Rather than making the decisions of which children to move to which class on my own, I established an annual working group of the lead teachers of our center. We met each year in the late spring or early summer to discuss and plan the September move-up. Since our center had two classrooms for each younger-age group, and three classrooms for the oldest children, ages three to five years, we had the opportunity to choose the best room for a child. We also had some flexibility in forming gender- and age-balanced classrooms as well as accommodating parents' preferences when we could.

In preparation for our meeting, I prepared index cards for each child in our program. The cards contained the child's name and date of birth. Cards were color coded to indicate the *current* room placement of each child. Each lead teacher received the stack of cards for all her current children. We set up several tables around the room on which were taped the room names of all our toddler and preschool classes. Each lead teacher then placed her cards by the classroom name on the tables where she wanted each child placed in September. In the process, with teachers moving about the room and distributing their cards, the teachers discussed children's placement with teachers of the target classrooms.

Teachers shared information and discussed each child. The program coordinators participated by sharing what they knew about children and/or families and giving their recommendations for placement. From time to time, we could step back and look at the configuration of each new group to determine whether some modification might be needed, and to make sure that no classroom had more children than it could accommodate. The two-hour meetings were pleasurable for everyone and an opportunity for everyone to work at being a decision maker. Usually the decisions made in the first meeting were revisited the next month and beyond until we were all generally satisfied with the new configuration of children and classes.

TEACHING YOURSELF TO LET GO

The most difficult part of learning inclusive decision making is learning when to let go and let others make the decisions. Initially it is easier to just "do it yourself." But you cannot continue to do everything. You shouldn't want to. You should be hiring and training people in your organization who want to make their own decisions. If you are the owner of a family child care home business, you probably have to make all the decisions for your program—you don't have a choice. But if there are other employees in your organization, you do have a choice. You will need to take the time required to train people if your teachers are not used to making many decisions.

Little by little, you will find that your teachers become empowered knowing they are responsible for what happens in their classroom. They know they are trusted and respected as early childhood educators. They can still come to you if they have tried to find a solution but are unable to reach agreement within their team, or have tried a solution that didn't fix the problem, or if they just need more information to help them make their decision. You'll soon find that you are no longer bogged down with making little decisions and responding to crises all day long. You now have time to work on the responsibilities for which you were hired and you may even find more time for enjoying this important work you do.

REFERENCE

Webster's New Collegiate Dictionary. (1980). Springfield, MA: Merriam-Webster.

Employee Performance Review Forms

Staff Pre-Conference Questionnaire

Dear

As you prepare for our planning conference, think about the following:

▤ What aspect of your job gives you the greatest personal satisfaction?

▤ What aspect of your job is most frustrating?

▤ What keeps you from being as effective as you would like to be in your position?

▤ If you had the power to change anything about your job, what would you change? Why would this be an improvement over existing conditions?

▤ What do you see yourself doing five years from now?

▤ What new skills or knowledge would you like to learn next year?

▤ How can I or other staff help you achieve your personal and professional goals?

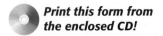

Print this form from the enclosed CD!

Goals Planning

Name of Teacher _____ Date _____

Your strengths in the classroom:

1. _____

2. _____

3. _____

Your areas for improvement:

1. _____

2. _____

3. _____

Your objectives for the year ahead:

1. _____

2. _____

3. _____

Supervisor signature _____ Date: _____

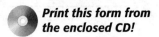

Print this form from the enclosed CD!

Staff Action Plan

Name of Teacher _____ Date _____

Objective 1 Activities:

1. _____ Complete by: _____

2. _____ Complete by: _____

3. _____ Complete by: _____

Resources needed:

Objective 2 Activities:

4. _____ Complete by: _____

5. _____ Complete by: _____

6. _____ Complete by: _____

Resources needed:

Objective 3 Activities:

7. _____ Complete by: _____

8. _____ Complete by: _____

9. _____ Complete by: _____

Resources needed:

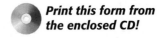 *Print this form from the enclosed CD!*

Spreadsheet Terminology

For those of you who have never used a spreadsheet, it will be helpful to understand some terminology used in the budget preparation and analyses in Chapters 4 and 5, and some basics of how spreadsheets work.

A computer spreadsheet is composed of cells, or boxes, of information. These cells are named by the intersection of the column and row names at their location. So, for example, a number located at the intersection of the column labeled "E" and Row 40, is located in Cell E40. A column label located in Column "B" and Row 8, is located in Cell B8.

A cell can contain a number, a word or words, or a mathematical formula. The cell name not only indicates the location of the information, but *it also stands for the information itself*. For Cell E18, we know the *location* is the intersection of Column E and Row 18, and we also know that E18 may contain a *value* of, for example, $270,000.

If the cell contains a formula, this formula will usually be hidden. What is shown in that cell is the *result* of that formula. In Figure B–1, Row 19, Columns D through G contain formulas that compute the dollars spent on payroll taxes as a percentage of the dollars spent on salaries. For example, in Cell G19 is the formula: Cell G18 times .09. You don't see the formula. What you do see is the result of this computation, or $247,227 times .09, which equals $22,050. In Cell G38 ("Total Expenses") is a formula to add all the numbers in Column G that are expenses: the sum of Cells G18 through G35.

In Figure B–2, what is hidden in each cell of the spreadsheet in Figure B–1 is displayed, and you can see examples of the different ways information is entered in a spreadsheet. Cells D9 through D12 contain fixed numbers. The cells for headings of row names and column names contain words. Other cells, such as E35 and D26, contain formulas.

Formulas in spreadsheets are very powerful tools. They allow you to perform instant calculations over and over. When you need to change figures somewhere in your budget, the cells in which you have formulas will automatically compute the new results. The same computations can be done manually, but it will always take you longer to do it by hand and you will probably have more mistakes than if you are using the computer.

Felton Family Preschool
Budget

	Estimated Current Year Results (12 Mos)	"Reasonable" Budget A	"Blue Sky" Budget B	"Conservative" Budget C
INCOME				
Tuition	315,000			
Fund-raising	7,000			
County Grant	20,000			
Other	2,000			
TOTAL INCOME	344,000			
EXPENSE				
Payroll Expense				
Salaries-Staff	247,227	270,000	275,000	247,227
Payroll Taxes	22,250	24,300	24,750	22,250
Worker's Comp	9,889	13,500	13,750	9,889
Staff Benefits				
Health Ins.	25,000	27,250	27,500	26,500
Dental Ins.	4,000	4,000	4,120	4,120
Education Allow.	875	875	875	875
Rent	4,800	4,800	4,800	4,800
Janitor	6,000	6,000	6,000	6,000
Insurance				
Accident	1,500	1,575	1,575	1,575
Directors Ins.	899	944	944	944
Liability	2,775	2,914	2,914	2,775
Supplies	14,053	17,566	17,566	11,242
Utilities	2,700	2,835	2,835	2,835
Capital Improvement	0	5,000	7,000	
TOTAL EXPENSES	341,969	376,559	382,629	341,033
SURPLUS (DEFICIT)	2,032			

FIGURE B–1 Felton Family Preschool Budget

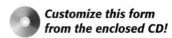

Customize this form from the enclosed CD!

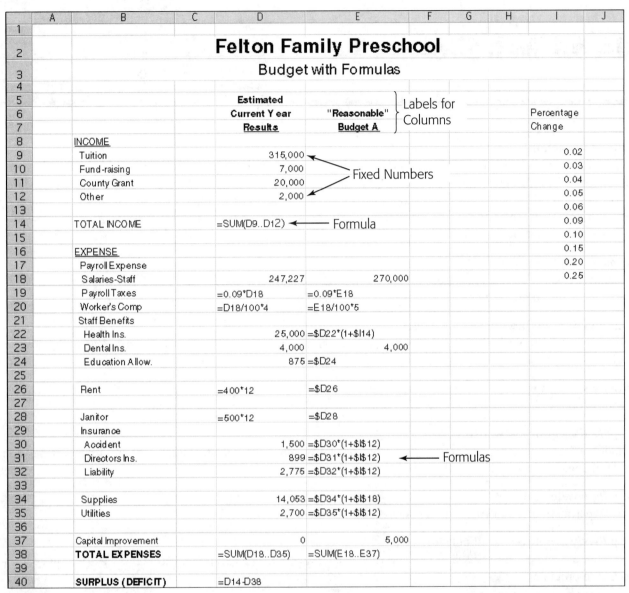

Felton Family Preschool
Budget with Formulas

		Estimated Current Year Results	"Reasonable" Budget A					Percentage Change	
INCOME									
Tuition		315,000						0.02	
Fund-raising		7,000						0.03	
County Grant		20,000						0.04	
Other		2,000						0.05	
								0.06	
TOTAL INCOME		=SUM(D9..D12)						0.09	
								0.10	
EXPENSE								0.15	
Payroll Expense								0.20	
Salaries-Staff		247,227	270,000					0.25	
Payroll Taxes		=0.09*D18	=0.09*E18						
Worker's Comp		=D18/100*4	=E18/100*5						
Staff Benefits									
Health Ins.		25,000	=$D22*(1+$I14)						
Dental Ins.		4,000	4,000						
Education Allow.		875	=$D24						
Rent		=400*12	=$D26						
Janitor		=500*12	=$D28						
Insurance									
Accident		1,500	=$D30*(1+$I$12)						
Directors Ins.		899	=$D31*(1+$I$12)						
Liability		2,775	=$D32*(1+$I$12)						
Supplies		14,053	=$D34*(1+$I$18)						
Utilities		2,700	=$D35*(1+$I$12)						
Capital Improvement		0	5,000						
TOTAL EXPENSES		=SUM(D18..D35)	=SUM(E18..E37)						
SURPLUS (DEFICIT)		=D14-D38							

Labels for Columns

Fixed Numbers

Formula

Formulas

FIGURE B–2 Felton Family Preschool Budget with Formulas

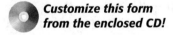

Customize this form from the enclosed CD!

Useful Web Sites

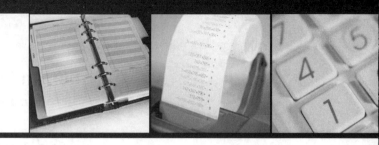

http://www.acf.dhhs.gov
U.S. Department of Health and Human Services, Administration for Children and Families. A site from which you can access various programs, including the Child Care Bureau. The Child Care Bureau provides funding for states, territories, and tribes, with assistance to low-income families, in accessing child care. Also provides information on start-up and improvement funding for child care, federal food programs, and Head Start. Also has a section on research and data related to child care.

http://www.bls.gov/oco
Contains the U.S. Department of Labor Occupational Handbook, 2002–2003 edition. Revised every two years. Child care workers listed under "personal care and service occupations."

http://www.BoundaryManagement.com
John Carver's company Web site. Help for nonprofit organizations in determining board management. Publications available.

http://www.ccw.org
Center for the Child Care Workforce. Statistics, studies, publications, some available online.

http://www.childcareaware.org
ChildCare Aware. Information (mostly for parents) on child care regulations, staff qualifications, teacher certification, and training.

http://www.dol.gov
U.S. Department of Labor Web site. Contains the employment law guide.

http://www.employeehandbookstore.com
Just what the name suggests: sells a PC or Mac version of an employee handbook with templates you can adapt to your own program.

http://www.naccrra.org
National Association of Child Care Referral and Resource Agencies (NACCRRA), which will guide you to your local referral and resource agency.

http://www.naeyc.org
National Association for the Education of Young Children.

http://www.nccic.org
National Child Care Information Center.

http://nrc.uchsc.edu
National Resource Center for Health and Safety in Child Care. Contains state licensing regulations for all states throughout the United States. Provides a link to NACCRRA Web site.

http://www.sampleemployeehandbook.com
Another site offering an employee handbook with templates (on CD for PCs only). An English-language or Spanish-language version is available, with specific information for all 50 states.

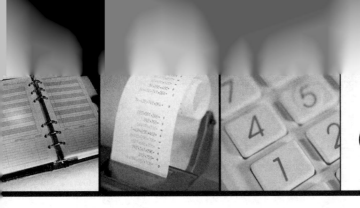

Glossary

Accounts Receivable—what your customers (includes parents and agencies you may bill for children's tuition) owe to you.

Accrual basis of accounting—a method of recording income when it is earned and expense information when the expense is incurred.

Bank reconciliation—the process of comparing and adjusting the bank account balances in your records to the bank account balances recorded by the bank.

Break-even budget—a budget where income is exactly equal to expense.

Buy-in—the process of earning commitment for a decision or process.

Capacity—the number of children you are allowed by licensing regulations to serve in your facility, or the number of children you decide to accommodate, whichever is lower.

Cash basis of accounting—a method of recording income when cash is received and expense information when cash is paid out.

Cell—in a computer spreadsheet, the location defined by the intersection of a row and a column.

Cleared transaction—a check, deposit, or electronic funds transfer that has been recorded in your bank account by your bank.

Close—the process of finalizing an accounting period.

Cost per child—total operating costs divided by the number of children in the facility.

Fiscal period—an accounting period that you define, such as your fiscal year from September 1 through August 31.

Fixed costs—Expenses that do not vary when your enrollment or staffing change.

Full cost of care—the amount of money it costs to care for one full-time child in your program.

Full cost of quality care—the amount of money it costs to care for one full-time child in your program when all the standards of quality care are met.

Inclusive decision making—The process of decision making that includes all those parties who have a stake in the outcome.

Living wage—the minimum wage rate that allows the wage earner to support her/his basic needs of food, clothing, and shelter.

Organizational climate—the "feel" of the working environment.

Overhead—annual administrative costs such as rent, insurance, administrative salaries, benefits, and taxes.

PTO—personal time off.

Reflection—the process of reflecting on one's own performance.

Soft money—income that is dispensed to you by an outside source, usually grant or fund-raising monies.

Variable costs—expenses that vary by the level of your enrollment and/or staffing.

Variance—the difference between two numbers; e.g., between budgeted expense and actual expense.

Index

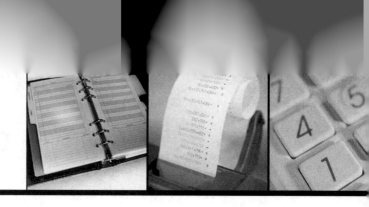

A

Accounting
    accrual basis of, vii, 102–103
    cash basis of, 102–103
Accounting software
    budget tracking within, 81
    types of, 114–115
    using, 115–118
Accounts receivable, 103
Accrual basis of accounting, vii
    cash basis of accounting
        versus, 102–103
Action plan, staff, 131
Administrative costs, 22
Administrative staff, 21–22
Administrators
    budgeting. *See* Budget
    creating a good work environment,
        6–8, 32
    management's needs from, 10–11
    management styles of. *See* Management
        styles
    role in decision making, 120–121
    staff relations. *See* Staff
    working with board of directors, 11
    working with families, 8–10
    working with managers, 10–12
    working with parent boards, 11–12
    working with parents, 8–10
    working with volunteer board of
        directors, 11–12
Advertising, 37–38
Average hourly wage rate, 91

B

Balance sheet, 110–111
    year-end, 119
Bank reconciliation, 104, 106
Bank statements, 104, 106
Benefits
    as budget component, 58
    as part of full cost of care, 22–25
    target salaries and benefits, 26
    types of, 35–37
Billing and payment ledger, 108
Billing records, 107–108
"Blue sky" budget, 52, 60, 133
Board of directors
    financial record keeping requests,
        101–102
    volunteer, 11–12
    working with, 11
Break-even budget, 50
Budget, 50–52
    "blue sky" budget. *See* "Blue sky" budget
    break-even budget, 50
    "conservative" budget. *See* "Conservative"
        budget
    expense components, 52–62
    expense line items, 52–53
    first-pass budget, 67

fiscal period, 50–52
fixed costs, 53
home child care, 55–56
inclusive decision making in, 123–124
monthly budgets, 72–79
as planning tool. *See* Planning tool,
    budget as
purpose of, 50
"reasonable" budget. *See* "Reasonable"
    budget
revenue components, 62–71
scenarios, 52, 60
spreadsheets. *See* Spreadsheets
staff salary and benefits, 58
start-up, 55–56
step one in building: estimating total
    expenses, 53–55
step two in building: estimating future
    expenses, 55–58
step three in building: constructing salary
    spreadsheet, 58–62
step four in building: estimating tuition
    revenue, 62–66
step five in building: balancing the
    budget, 66–71
tracking within accounting software, 81
using. *See* Planning tool, budget as
variable costs, 53
variances, 51
Buy-in, 6

C

Capacity, 13–14
    determination of, 14–15
    flexibility in maintaining, 15
    maintaining high enrollment, 16–18
    NAEYC accreditation guidelines, 14–15
    state licensing guidelines, 14–15
Cash basis of accounting, accrual basis of
    accounting versus, 102–103
Cash reserves, 87
CCW. *See* Center for the Child Care
    Workforce (CCW)
Cells, 58, 132
Center for the Child Care Workforce
    (CCW), 5
    salary survey, 33
Chart of accounts, 115–117
Check register, 104, 105, 112
Child care administrator. *See* Administrator
Child care management software, 114
Cleared transaction, 117
Close, 104, 118
Communication with parents, 8–9
Compensation package, 33–37
Computers
    software. *See* Software
    spreadsheets. *See* Spreadsheets
"Conservative" budget, 52, 60, 133
Controlling managers, 2
Cost per child, 22–25
Cost savings, 95, 100

D

Decision making
    administrator's role in, 120–121
    inclusive. *See* Inclusive decision making
    staff participation in, 6, 49, 121–122
Deficits, reducing, 89–100
Disciplining staff, 6, 46–47
Disseminating information to staff, 6–8
Documents, financial record keeping,
    103–111
    balance sheet, 110–111
    bank reconciliation, 104, 106
    bank statements, 104, 106
    billing records, 107–108
    check register, 104, 105, 112
    computer software. *See* Software
    computer spreadsheets, 111, 113
    income and expense statement,
        109–110
    income register, 106–107
    manual maintenance system, 111
    methods for maintaining, 111–118
    payroll records, 109
    profit and loss statement, 109–110, 113
    software. *See* Software
Doer, 4

E

Employee handbooks, 42
Enrollment
    capacity. *See* Capacity
    full enrollment, 13
    importance of, 13–14
    maintaining high enrollment, 16–18
    relationship to staffing, 14
    as revenue component in budget, 62
Expense line items in budget, 52–53
Expenses, 22–25
    benefits. *See* Benefits
    as component of budget, 52–62
    salaries. *See* Salaries
    tracking month-to-month, 79–83

F

Families. *See also* Parents
    communication with enrolled, 17–18
    making program a good place for, 8–9
    working with, 8–10
Feeler, 4
Fees, tuition. *See* Tuition fees
Fee structure, determining, 18–30
    data used in, 29–30
    full cost of care. *See* Full cost of care
    full-time care, 28–29
    hourly rate, 19
    market rate comparison, 19
    part-time care, 28–29
File notes for staff review, 125
Financial record keeping
    benefits of, 102, 118
    chart of accounts, 115–117

documents. *See* Documents, financial
  record keeping
fiscal year-end, 118–119
legal requirements, 101
management's requirements, 101–102
necessary documents. *See* Documents,
  financial record keeping
Finding qualified staff, advertisements
  for, 37–39
First-pass budget, 67
Fiscal period, 50–52
Fiscal year-end, 118–119
Fixed costs, 53
Flexibility in enrollment capacity, 15
Full cost of care, 19–25
  administrative costs, 22
  administrative staff, 21–22
  computing, 28
  cost per child, 22–25
  determining, 22–25
  expenses, 22–25
  other staff, 21–22
  overhead, 22
  teachers and staffing ratios, 19–21
Full cost of quality care, 25–28
  computing, 27
  defined, 25
  qualifications, 25
Full enrollment, 13
Full-time care, part-time care versus, 28–29

G

Goals planning template, 126, 130

H

Handbooks, employee, 42
Health insurance, 36–37
Hiring process
  inclusive decision making in, 40–41
  interviews, 39–40
  making hiring decision, 40–41
  offer letter, 41–42
Home child care budgets, 55–56
Hourly rate, 19

I

Inclusive decision making
  in budgeting, 123–124
  in child care environment, 122–123
  defined, 122
  effect of, 123
  examples of, 123–127
  in hiring process, 40–41
  learning to let go, 127
  in moving children, 124, 126–127
  in performance reviews, 124
Income. *See* Revenue
Income and expense statement, 109–110
Income register, 106–107
Insurance
  as budget item, 53
  health, 36–37
  types of, 53
Internet sites, useful, 135
Interviewing job applicants, 39–40
Intuitor, 4

J

Job descriptions
  purpose of, 42–43
  sample, 44, 45
Job fairs, 38

L

Leadership styles, 2–3
Living wage, 26

M

Maintaining high enrollment, 16–18
Management's needs from child care
  administrator, 10–11
Management styles, 1–5
  development of, 3–4
  effect of personality on, 4–5
  flexibility and fluidity with employees, 2
  organizational climate, 2, 6–8
  reflection, 4–5
  research on, 1–3
  spectrum of, 3
  staff relations. *See* Staff
  types of, 2–3
  uniqueness in, 4–5
  working with families, 8–10
  working with managers, 10–12
  working with parents, 8–10
Managers, working with, 10–12
Manual maintenance system for financial
  records, 111
Market rate comparison, 19
Meeting time, staff, 48–49
Monthly budgets, 72–79
Moving children, inclusive decision making
  in, 124, 126–127
My Bookkeeper®, 114

N

NAEYC. *See* National Association for the
  Education of Young Children (NAEYC)
National Association for the Education of
  Young Children (NAEYC), 14–15
Negative variance, 88

O

Offer letter, 41–42
Open houses, 38
Organizational climate, 2, 6–8
Orientation for new staff, 47–48
Overhead, 22. *See also* Expenses

P

Parent boards, working with, 11–12
Parents. *See also* Families
  communication with, 8–9
  needs of, 8
  recruiting, 11–12
  working with, 8–10
Parent survey, 16, 17
Part-time care, full-time care versus, 28–29
Payroll records, 109
Peachtree First Accounting®, 115
Performance reviews, 43, 46
  inclusive decision making in, 124
Permissive managers, 2
Personality styles, 4
Personal time off (PTO), 36
Personnel policies and procedures
  disciplining staff, 46–47
  employee handbook, 42
  job descriptions. *See* Job descriptions
Planning tool, budget as
  average hourly wage rate, 91
  estimating monthly budget amounts,
    72–79
  estimating salaries, 74–77
  estimating tuition revenue, 77–79

reducing deficits, 89–100
tracking revenue and expense
  month-to-month, 79–83
using the budget, 72
variances. *See* Variances
Pre-conference questionnaire, staff, 125, 129
Preparation and meeting time, staff, 48–49
Professional development program, 48
Profit and loss statement, 109–110, 113
  year-end, 119
PTO. *See* Personal time off (PTO)

Q

QuickBooks®, 114, 115, 117

R

"Reasonable" budget, 52, 60, 133
Recognition programs, staff, 48
Record keeping, financial. *See* Financial record
  keeping
Reflection, 4–5
Reggio Emilia curriculum, 9
Revenue
  enrollment as source of, 13
  sources of, 62
  tracking month-to-month, 79–83
  tuition fees used in estimating, 62–66,
    77–79
Revenue components of budget, 62–71

S

Salaries. *See also* Wages
  and benefits, 22–25
  as budget component, 58
  designing structure for staff, 33–35
  estimating for budgeting purposes,
    74–77
  living wage, 26
  as overhead, 22
  spreadsheet, 21, 58–62
  target salaries and benefits, 26–27
Soft money, 62
Software
  accounting. *See* Accounting software
  budget tracking within accounting, 81
  child care management, 114
  financial record keeping, 113–118
Spreadsheets
  cells, 58, 132
  financial record keeping maintained
    in, 111, 113
  monthly budget, 79, 80
  salary, 21, 58–62
  samples, 133–134
  terminology for, 132
  tuition estimate, 63–66, 69
  working with, 56–57
  working with budget, 57–58
Staff
  administrative, 21–22
  being good to, 5
  benefits. *See* Benefits
  buy-in, 6
  caring about, 5
  disciplining, 6
  disseminating information to, 6–8
  file notes for review, 125
  finding qualified, 37–39
  hiring process. *See* Hiring process
  knowledge of, 5–6
  orientation, 47–48
  participation in decision making.
    See Decision making

Staff (*Continued*)
  performance of, 6
  performance reviews. *See* Performance
    reviews
  personnel policies and procedures.
    See Personnel policies and
    procedures
  preparation and meeting time, 48–49
  professional development
    program, 48
  recognition programs, 48
  reducing to save costs, 95, 100
  salaries. *See* Salaries
  salary spreadsheet, 21, 58–62
  wages. *See* Wages
Staff action plan, 131
Staffing
  creating a good work environment,
    6–8, 32
  factors determining, 32–37
  hiring process. *See* Hiring process
  ratios, 19–21
  relationship of enrollment to, 14
Staffing pattern chart, 20
Staff performance, ways to improve, 6
Staff pre-conference questionnaire,
    125, 129
Start-up budgets, 55–56

Staying ahead of falling enrollment,
    16–18
Storyboard presentations, 9

T

Target salaries and benefits, 26–27
Tax returns, year-end, 119
Teachers and staffing ratios, 19–21
Thinker, 4
Tracking revenue and expense
    month-to-month, 79–83
Tuition fees, 18–30
  annual review of, 30
  estimating revenue from, 62–66,
    77–79
  fee structure. *See* Fee structure,
    determining
  full cost of care. *See* Full cost of care
  full cost of quality care. *See* Full cost of
    quality care
  full-time care, 28–29
  increasing, 100
  part-time care, 28–29
  spreadsheets for estimating, 63–66, 69

U

Useful Web sites, 135

V

Variable costs, 53
Variances, 51
  in income and expense, 80
  negative, 88
  operations after seven months, 85–89
  operations at the end of two months,
    83–85
  understanding, 83–100
Volunteer board of directors, 11–12

W

Wage grids, 33, 34
Wage matrix, 34, 35
Wages
  average hourly wage rate, 91
  designing structure for staff, 33–35
  living wage, 26
Waiting lists, 18
Web sites, useful, 135
Word of mouth, 38–39
Work environment, creating a good, 6–8, 32

Y

Year-end balance sheet, 119
Year-end profit and loss statement, 119
Year-end tax returns, 119